*the Run of*
*My Life*

# the Run of My Life

## A MEMOIR OF HEALING

### ROCHELLE FINZEL

BOLD
STORY
PRESS

CHEVY CHASE, MD

Bold Story Press, Chevy Chase, MD 20815
www.boldstorypress.com

First edition: September 2024
Library of Congress Control Number: 2023916851

ISBN: 978-1-954805-60-6 (paperback)
ISBN: 978-1-954805-61-3 (e-book)

Cover and interior design by Karen Polaski
Author photo by Alan Fisser

Printed in the United States of America
10   9   8   7   6   5   4   3   2   1

To my angel, John.
And my true love, Alan.

# Contents

# one

# Sitting on Top

I imagined my next trip in a small box; my ashes and bone fragments sloshing around as my boyfriend carefully climbs the steep ridge, holding onto the thick steel chains for support. He will take a small pinch of dust and toss it into the wind, leaving behind a speck of me in this gorgeous landscape.

I breathed in the fresh desert air from my perch atop this iconic cliff. Angel's Landing felt appropriate for my final voyage. The views stretched for miles, and I studied the curves of the Virgin River as it snaked its way through the canyon and slipped around a wall of rock. I removed my backpack and sat down; the weight shifting from my shoulders to the heavy pit in my stomach.

I knew I was dying. The four women in white coats. All the questions about my previous cancer. The lumps that kept popping up everywhere on my body, from the little purplish spot on my collarbone to the sand dollar-sized globs on my back. Not to mention how freaking tired I felt.

I glanced over at Alan and a surge of sorrow erupted from the soles of my feet to the top of my head. No more multiple summit hiking days, bushwhacking straight up steep slopes, and scrambling across rocky ridges; or the best, glissading down slopes on our butts over spring snow, laughing like school children. No more spontaneous mobile Wine Wednesdays sipping out of our stainless-steel cups and eating cheese and crackers from the tiny cutting board on the car's dashboard after an evening hike. No more ski trips and afternoon beers on the patio.

My favorite song in college was "Ironic" by Alanis Morrisette. My life was becoming a new lyric. "It's like achieving your dream life, and then getting a death sentence . . . ."

I stared at the sandstone walls lining the canyon, amazed at their size. Massive hunks of rock guarded the tiny river that separated the towering structures. It was a gorgeous display of Mother Nature's wonder, and made me want to see more of her beauty and to continue to feel the freedom and pure joy I felt outdoors, witnessing the grandeur of this earthly life.

The park's name, Zion, is ancient Hebrew for "sanctuary" or "refuge." Zion features steep walls and biblical monikers for its rock formations. I knew I was here to lay my soul to rest; to be in this canyon cathedral and pray before its towering altars of stone. The gentle breeze and swooping ravens called me forth to make peace with this life and its mysteries.

Our first and last vacation.

Thick clouds shrouded the early morning sun, creating a dull gray backdrop to the burnt orange rock formations outside our hotel window. It was day five of our week-long Utah vacation. My body ached as I rolled over in bed to check the time. I ran a marathon the day we left for Utah. I had hoped to run fast enough to meet the time standard to qualify for the coveted Boston Marathon, but unfortunately, I came up short of that goal. I was exhausted. Luckily, we weren't in a hurry, so I pulled my sore knees to my chest and curled up in the fetal position. I tried to go back to sleep, but my mind was awake enough to remember that I had biopsy results waiting for me from the lumps on my back and neck. How much of my exhaustion was from running, and how much was hidden inside those mysterious lumps? The wave of fear washed over me; its force like a punch in the gut knocking the wind out of me. I tucked my hand under my armpit and felt the soft fleshy nodule. It was still there. And a little tender. I cupped my breast, wondering if my little boobs were going to be gone soon.

I closed my eyes and tried to quiet my thoughts, willing myself to focus on my breath and listen to the sound of the birds chirping outside. I wanted to hear anything other than the voices of death that kept whispering in my ear.

It was no use. My mind was back in control after its night of fitful dreams. And my bladder was full. I gingerly slid out from under the covers and limped to the bathroom, cursing the throbbing pain in my knee.

Alan was sitting on the side of the bed when I came out. I sidled up behind him and kissed his neck. I wanted to bury my body in his strong arms and curl back up in bed, but I also wanted to get out and get moving. The dark motel room only amplified my fears and gave them space to roam. A confined space with nowhere for me to hide.

"Do you want to grab some breakfast at that diner down the street?" Alan asked. "I'm sick of cereal."

"Yeah, that sounds good to me. I could go for some eggs and real coffee."

We sat in a nice booth at the old diner that was decorated in western fashion. Ranch and cowboy paraphernalia adorned the walls. Animal heads stared back at me as I tried to concentrate on what Alan was saying, and ignore the chorus of frightened voices in my head.

Clouds. Rain. Darkness. With all the ravens flying about and Zion's stark towering rock walls, the overcast skies made the location feel more like a dungeon than a beautiful canyon.

"What time do you think we'll get to Bryce?" I asked, trying desperately to make small talk.

"I guess there's no rush. We aren't planning to hike, so we can take our time."

I nodded, happy that we could slow down but afraid of my growing exhaustion. I tried to keep up and not whine about my aching knees, but yesterday's bow out on the last hike clearly indicated that I needed a break.

We loaded the last bag in the car and started the drive to Bryce Canyon. A light drizzle provided just enough moisture to seep into the canyon wall's sandstone, deepening its natural hue. I stared out the window and studied the massive rock formations as we headed out of the park, curving along the same Coliseum-like structure, a natural amphitheater before we entered the tunnel. Claustrophobia immediately gripped me, and I saw the tunnel collapsing, swallowing us into the rock. I held my breath and willed the walls to withstand the forces pressing on it. I exhaled as we finally exited the tunnel into the dim light.

The landscape opened as we drove higher up the mesa, winding around miniature versions of the pink and ivory stone towers of the park. The rocks flattened slightly, their shades making them appear as giant ice cream cones swirling down to the ground. The canyon wall's shapes made it easy to imagine the waves and water that flowed through millions of years ago. This grand scale of erosion and geologic transformation seemed like a museum of natural art; the structure and composition unique and abstract. Around every bend something caught my eye. The single juniper tree sticking out of the rock, hundreds of feet above the ground with no other green plant life in sight. The winding washes of dry sand that would turn into raging rivers in a rainstorm. The yucca plants, piñon pine trees, and pockets of bright red Paintbrush flowers adding flashes of color and contrast to the smooth and pale rocks.

I focused on every scene before me, memorizing its features and noting every detail, trying to avoid staring at my phone in my lap. My phone hadn't rung since we left Denver. I thought the doctor would have called by now.

"You haven't heard anything yet?" Alan asked.

"No. I know we haven't had good service, but I don't have any messages. I wish he'd just call."

"Me too."

We continued in silence, both lost in our own thoughts. I tried to imagine what he must be thinking. That his girlfriend is crazy for being such a worried mess about a couple lumps, or that he was kicking himself for dating a girl who'd been diagnosed with cancer before. Perhaps he was just as scared and worried as his crazy cancer girlfriend sitting next to him.

I just imagined death and suffering. I was fine with dying, but I couldn't handle the suffering.

I had watched my sister get sick and go through hell with leukemia when she was a teenager. Her bald head covered in purple marks, and the plastic wastebasket that served as her puke bucket during our one and only family road trip to New Mexico. It all looked so awful to me. I hated puking.

I remembered the old Ecuadorian man in the hospital for Hanson's disease (leprosy) patients where I volunteered after college. He died alone after years of isolation from his family. I had visited him nearly every day before he died. I held his hand, his leathery skin like that of a snake, and his sharp bones jutting out of his skin like jagged rocks. I expected him to literally waste away and turn into a flat mass of flesh. His breathing slowing, the shine in his eyes dimming, which he eventually stopped opening.

I recalled the hospice visit to see Alan's friend in her final days. Such a contrast to the first time I met her, when she wore a bandana turban and smiled widely as she spoke of her shopping escapades with her children. One month later, she lay in the bed lifeless, her family seated closely in chairs surrounding her bed. Quiet, with their eyes full of sadness. I watched her husband wipe away his tears, as he shook his head outside her room trying to comprehend life without her.

I looked out the car's window, scanning the rocky landscape for something to hold onto, like the lone bush clinging to the rock wall. *Let me hang on.*

My silent pleas were interrupted, however, by the sound of my phone ringing. I looked at Alan and then down at its screen, the number and caller ID confirming it was my doctor. I took a deep breath and hit the button nervously, bringing the phone to my ear.

"Hello, this is Rochelle."

"Rochelle, this is Dr. Barkley. How are you?"

"I'm fine, how are you?"

"I'm calling to let you know the results of your biopsy."

Slight pause.

"It's not good news."

Another pause.

"The lumps are melanoma."

My mind immediately knew what that meant. The cancer had spread. Stage four melanoma. No chances of survival. I was going to die, and I was going to die fast. My premonitions come to fruition. My next trip to Angel's Landing would be in a box, full of dust and bone fragments.

"We want you to have a PET scan and an MRI of your brain. We don't think it has spread to your brain, but we just want to make sure."

"Ok," I stammered. "When do we need to do those? I mean, I'm on vacation, do you think anything needs to be done tomorrow? Or can it wait until I am back in town on Monday?" *Or never. Can this just wait?*

"Oh, you are still out of town. I know they said you were going on vacation. I don't think it would make a difference if you waited until Monday. Can I schedule it for you?"

"Would you? That would be great." I knew it had to be bad when he offered to schedule the appointment for me.

"Ok, let me make some calls, and then I'll get back to you."

Another pause.

"I'm very sorry, Rochelle."

"It's OK. Thanks, doctor, for making the appointments. I really appreciate it."

"You're welcome," he said.

I knew that his making of that appointment was more about his need to do something. His need to help fix my problem. He told me just two weeks ago that it wasn't melanoma. And now he had to call me and contradict himself. I almost felt bad for him.

I hit the end call button and turned to Alan, who had pulled the car over to the shoulder of the road. He was the one thing in my life I was not ready to leave. The one person I finally allowed myself to love and to love me back. The man who healed me of past wounds so deep that I had lost hope of curing. I grabbed him around the neck and burrowed my head into his shoulder.

"I don't want to die."

He wrapped me in his arms and gently stroked my hair. "I'm sorry, honey."

I leaned back into my seat, and we sat in silence holding hands. I stared at the big sandstone bridge in front of us, trying to process what the doctor just told me. I repeated his words to Alan. The lumps are melanoma, I need to do a PET scan and an MRI. The doctor will schedule those for me and call me back.

I didn't mention anything about what it really means. This is metastatic melanoma. It kills—fast. I kept that to myself, knowing he would find out soon enough. Or he could leave, exiting before he had to see me like his friend in hospice. Before he would grieve like her sobbing husband.

Alan looked over at me and asked what we should do now. I looked back at him, my eyes focused on his. "We're on vacation. Let's go to Bryce."

A smile crept across his face. "I'm glad that's your answer." We pulled back out onto the road as the rain began falling.

I kept thinking he should go home now. Drive fast to Denver and leave me and my mess behind. But at the same time, I was so glad that he was with me. Honestly, I really never wanted him to leave.

I had hoped this vacation would be good for us. An escape from our mutually stressful lives. My job was pulling me in numerous directions with none of them good. He had been taking care of his mom after her recent fall and broken hip. We both needed a break. I had hoped it would bring back the carefree days of our first months of dating. Days when our biggest problems were figuring out which mountain to climb, on what trails, and whether we'd eat peanut butter and jelly sandwiches at the top or just prepackaged energy bars and jerky. I wanted this to be an easy week. Time to rest and rejuvenate. To explore a new part of the country; places I've wanted to visit since seeing them in pictures taken 20 years ago by my mother's friend. This was not exactly how I imagined our carefree first vacation to be. Nor had I imagined that it could be our last.

We passed the park's entrance gates and followed the road through the ponderosa pines until we reached the first viewpoint. We turned left and pulled into the very full parking lot. Tourists were milling about with large cameras around their necks, as children were tugging at their legs. We slipped into our rain jackets to keep out the rain falling from the sky and somberly walked hand in hand to the edge. I walked around in a fog, weaving my way through the crowds with their big cameras and umbrellas. My ears barely registered their Oohs and Ahhs trying to penetrate my cloudy brain. Everyone was smiling and laughing despite the raindrops. I felt a little out of place with my red puffy eyes and very heavy heart.

We neared the large cement viewing platform and metal fence, and suddenly the brown and green of the forest dropped away into an oasis of orange and white. Like a sea of floating candles—white flames atop fantastically shaped fire-orange bases. The drizzle soaking into the rocks intensified their color and brightness as they shone amidst the cloudy gray. They appeared to be lit from inside, casting their glow throughout the canyon.

I looked around and felt the light's power filling the cracks of doom and darkness that permeated my soul and flew through Zion's gothic cathedral with her black ravens and iron-stained walls. The magical scene appeared surreal with its fantastical shapes and colors. I nearly laughed out loud at the stark contrast between the dungeon of Zion and this fairyland of Bryce. I might be dying, but this was the most joyful symbol of life that I had ever witnessed. The canyon glowed, its hue a giant smiley face in the ground.

I started to pull my camera out of my pocket and realized that any pictures I took would end up in a box for someone else to sort. My memories would have to go with me. I took photos in my mind, capturing the imaginary sunken ship off in the distance, the chicken head atop the tower to my right, and the window just below the rim.

The magical beauty of this canyon flicked a switch inside and reminded me that there was still life to live. I made my peace with dying at the altars of Zion, but for now I was living. Living and breathing amid the most stunningly unique rock formations and vibrant colors. Not only was I *not* dead, but I was finally living the life of my dreams, vacationing with a man who shared the same awe and gratitude for nature's powerful beauty. Someone who loved me as much as I loved him.

*two*

---

# Learning to Climb

T welve years earlier, I had a big dark spot on the back of my leg that grew and bled, and not surprisingly turned out to be melanoma. It was my first cancer diagnosis. I've always wondered if stress played a role in that first tumor. I had been unhappy at my job then, and I certainly felt plenty of dissatisfaction in my now current position.

In recent gatherings with friends, I'd found myself unable to hide my frustration.

"How's your job?" my friend asked, as we plodded along the trail, sunlight streaming through the conifer forest.

"Ugh, it's killing me," I told her. "I'm getting sick of doing my boss's job as well as my own." I then explained the latest drama when the financial director asked if I knew why the boss hadn't filed a report on

13

time, and then told me that *I* needed to produce and file it instead.

Scenes like this ran through my head as we walked along, and I could feel my pace quicken. I didn't like to think about work on the weekends, so I stomped the ground a few times and changed the subject.

I had been warned by one of the hiring managers about the unspoken roles of my job. She mentioned it during my final interview for the position. It had been a beautiful summer day, and I glanced down at my watch as the thin man led me down the hall and past pictures of state capitols adorning the walls as well as the rotunda that looked downward on the lobby, a symbol of the political world in which the organization operated and its national scope. It was a world I had long wanted to enter.

Ever since my college internship when I had worked with young moms struggling to get by in poor neighborhoods, I wanted to do something bigger to help them. One-on-one social work wasn't satisfying once I saw firsthand the systems and policies that made life harder rather than easier for my clients. Changing policy and public perception felt more important. It was a way to make a bigger change for more people rather than helping one person at a time.

I had become aware of this national organization when interviewing for my previous positions, and knew of its prestige and credibility. I would be working directly with policymakers and state agency directors from across the country in a bipartisan and educational role. It was a dream job that included travel and connection to leading researchers and thought leaders on poverty and policy. After working at the community level, moving up to state and national politics was a big step. Although I felt like a dog drooling expectantly for a bite of steak on a plate, I tried to control my excitement and play it cool with all the interviewers and potential colleagues.

I had arrived for the interview at nine that morning, and it was now nearly three in the afternoon. The policy director knocked on the door of a spacious window-lined office, and from around the corner the chief operating officer appeared. She wore black pants and a simple top, with her hair cut short. He introduced us, and she welcomed me to sit at the round table next to her desk. She seemed friendly and asked where I was from and how the rest of the interviews had gone.

We settled into the usual interview questions: Why I wanted the job, and what qualified me. I answered her with the same responses I'd given all the previous interviewers and potential co-workers. She nodded and seemed pleased with my answers.

She asked if I'd be moving, and what sort of timeline I'd need before starting the position. I was optimistic about my chances as she described the benefits and travel commitments, and I felt a little flutter of excitement in my stomach.

"I have one last question," she said.

She placed her hands on the table, pulling herself in closer and leaning towards me. Her face took on a serious expression as she told me the manager I'd be working for was known to be difficult. In fact, the person who I would be replacing had left because she could no longer tolerate working for him. The previous employee explained that reasoning to the leadership team, so they were all aware of the challenges. Yet, they'd made it clear they weren't going to do anything about it. "If you take this job, that is who you would be dealing with. We all know, so it's not worth complaining about it. Do you think you can handle it?" she asked, as she leaned back in her chair and crossed her arms.

My body tensed up as her eyes bore into me, waiting for an answer. I uncrossed my legs, sat up ramrod straight in my chair, and returned her gaze. "I worked for an Army colonel; I think I can handle it."

She smiled.

I'd worked for more than one difficult boss before. In my first real job out of college, the woman I worked for had determined my pay based on my marital status. I was single and childless, so I got paid less than my married female colleague with children, even though we had the same job. In my next position at a community nonprofit, my boss believed that the way to make you a better employee was to get your nose bloodied. Another had liked to pit colleagues against one another and play manipulative games.

In my first five years of professional experience, I began to realize that many managers were given that title *not* because they were good at leading people, but as a reward for their loyalty or expertise. In my job with the boss who liked to pit members of his staff against one another, some of my colleagues and I expressed our concerns to our boss's superiors. The following year, the boss laid me off. I knew the layoff wasn't retaliation, but

I certainly got the message that trying to get rid of a toxic boss could backfire.

I had learned to go along in order to get along in the working world. Speaking up wasn't worth it, so I kept my head down and worked hard. I believed the more you suffered, the greater the glory. It was practically our family motto. If we'd a family crest, it would have been of a person with their back bent, arms out, prostrate to whatever master who was to be served. Agreeing to the terms set out by the COO for this potential job came easily.

Two days later, I arrived home to a message from my soon-to-be boss. His voice was kind and inviting, as he said he'd like to offer me the job. I was the perfect candidate, and he asked me to return his call.

I was born and raised a rule follower; my parents were devout Catholics and hardworking farmers who taught their children to honor our word, do our work, and give thanks to God. Service and sacrifice. Suffering and humility.

The COO had stated the rules. I just needed to follow them. Besides, her warning became a challenge—an opportunity to do something that no one else seemed able to do: Work with a jerk. Hell, I'd been working with arrogant or insecure jackasses (depending on your perspective) since my first professional position. I knew how to put up and shut up, and still get the job done. I would be the one to break the mold; I would not quit because of a difficult boss. And I certainly wouldn't complain. I'd learned that lesson the hard way.

I had learned to be a quiet dutiful helper when I was 11 years old. On a rainy spring afternoon in 1985, a month before the end of my fifth-grade year, I rode the bus home by myself. My brother, who was 17, had driven to school, while my older 15-year-old sister Jolene had stayed home sick, and my two younger sisters were with a neighbor. I quickly walked down the sidewalk to our house and hopped onto the covered porch to get out of the drizzle. No one was around. I opened the door, dropped my white and red schoolbag on the floor, and headed to the kitchen. As usual, a note was left behind. The familiar cursive of my mother's handwriting was scrawled across the scrap of paper on the kitchen table.

*"Took Jolene to Iowa City. The doctors think she has leukemia."*

At the bottom of the note, she had added: *Put away the dishes.*

Jolene had been sick for weeks. We all thought it was just a bad virus; one doctor thought it was mono. Standing alone in our kitchen, I read my mother's words over again, hoping they would change. I didn't know what leukemia was, but to an 11-year-old it sounded scary.

I turned toward the stairs and walked up to the hallway where our 1978 set of faux leatherbound World Book Encyclopedias were stacked on a wooden shelf. I picked up the thick book with "L" on the spine and flipped through until I found the entry for leukemia; a few dense paragraphs about a blood disorder with scientific terms that I didn't understand. But one sentence stood out as if in bold and capital letters:

*Most people die from this disease of the white blood cells.*

I couldn't take my eyes off those words. I imagined never seeing my sister again. Would I sit on a couch in a room full of people as my sister lay dead in a casket across the hall, like my friend, Nichole, whose father died just a few months ago? My knees buckled. I sat down on the shag carpet and crossed my legs, the encyclopedia open and resting on my knees. I read the entry over and over, trying to find hope in the rest of the medical jargon. The house felt like a dungeon on that dreary April day. The silence amplified my fears in the empty house.

I slammed the volume shut and stood up, shoving the encyclopedia into its gap between J–K and M. Sliding my hand along the wooden banister, I walked downstairs and decided to call Nichole. Her father died in a tragic accident two months before, and I'd held her hand and listened as she cried, told me stories about him, and recounted images of him visiting in her dreams. She was the only one who I felt could relate.

I picked up the ivory phone receiver and listened. Thankfully the old lady who shared our party phone line wasn't swapping gossip, so I heard the familiar dial tone. I slowly dialed each number, hesitating before each one. By the time I dialed all the numbers, my hands were shaking and I could barely hold the receiver to my ear. I waited as it rang a few times, and my heart thumped furiously in my chest.

"Hello," my friend said. I heard the familiar sound of her sweet voice and immediately started bawling.

"It's me . . . Rochelle," I said between sobs. "The doctors . . . they think . . . Jolene . . . has leukemia."

I wailed into the phone, holding on to the kitchen table for support.

"What did you say? I can't understand you!"

I heard her whisper, "It's OK," over and over. I cried even harder, trying to catch my breath and stop my chest from heaving. I wiped the snot from my face, took a deep breath inward, and blurted out again, "The doctors think Jolene has leukemia," as I choked on another body-shaking sob.

"How do you know?"

I gulped and sputtered, "They left me a note."

"Who did? What did it say?"

"My parents," I whimpered. I picked up the note and read it to her, leaving out the part about dish duty.

She replied, "It says the doctors *think* it could be leukemia. They could be wrong. Doctors are wrong all the time." She told me about someone whose doctors thought they had a disease, but it turned out that they didn't. She kept reassuring me that it was going to be OK.

The confidence exuded in Nichole's voice calmed the pounding of my heart. My shoulders stopped shaking, and my lip stopped quivering. My sobs subsided, and the tears slowly quit running down my cheeks. I wiped my face with the back of my sleeve and rubbed my eyes.

"You're right," I stuttered.

I don't remember what else I said, or if I even thanked her for talking me off the ledge that afternoon. For reassuring me that it would be OK, and for stepping into my pain. She had just lost her father, and I was afraid I would lose my sister. I knew Nichole would be the only one who could possibly understand.

I hoped I wasn't going to be the next one sitting in a funeral home.

I hung up the phone and looked outside. The rain had stopped. I didn't bother changing out of my school uniform, and instead walked out onto the porch and down the sidewalk to our garage. I opened the door and picked up the basketball, dribbling it out onto the gravel driveway. I stood and stared at the metal hoop and wooden backboard. Taking a deep breath, I arced the ball up and through the net. With each shot, I moved a little faster until I was driving hard to the basket and attempting alley-oop shots and reverse layups under the basket like my brother taught me. I looked down towards the hog shed, hoping to see his blonde hair, goofy smile, and big teeth. He had to be somewhere on the farm, but I saw and heard no one.

I was an only child that day, alone and on my own. My brother and sisters weren't around, and Jolene and my parents were 2 hours away in a hospital room. I put all my fear and worry into throwing that basketball. I drove towards the hoop and heaved the ball from long range. My emotions had nowhere else to go, and no one to catch them. That day, I learned to handle bad news by myself, and to channel my emotions into physical activity. Thankfully, Nichole answered the phone.

---

Doctors confirmed my sister's diagnosis on that dreary April day. Her illness happened to coincide with one of the busiest times on the farm—planting season. Mom spent most of her time at the hospital when my sister started chemo, while my dad remained on the farm to tend to the chores as well as us kids. That year he'd signed a last-minute contract on a patch of ground, and it needed to be planted. Most crops were planted already, and with all the travel back and forth, time was running out.

One quintessential Iowa spring morning, I sat on the porch in the warm light admiring the colorful tulips that bordered the porch. The soft green lawn stretched out like a plush carpet up to the road. I listened to the birds chirping and watched robins flit around the yard, stopping to peck the ground for worms and insects. I rocked the porch swing back and forth, in and out of the shade from the porch's overhang and into the sunshine. I stuck my feet out and tried to keep my toes in the light as I rocked back towards the house.

The quiet did not last long. Soon cars were pulling into the driveway, their tires crunching on the gravel, as they parked one next to the other until the entire space was filled with the familiar vehicles of my neighbors. Wood-paneled station wagons and solid color sedans, all covered in various layers of dust. No cars stayed clean for long on our rural dusty roads.

Tractors chugged along the road from both directions, big red Internationals and sleek green John Deeres. They pulled planters and disks and all manners of equipment. Some turned south into the cornfield across the road, while others rolled behind the corn bin and into the northern fields. I didn't know how they knew where to go or what to plant, but they all drove along as if they had planted the ground before. It was an impressive sight to watch as the tractors marched across the fields.

Women got out of the cars, loaded with bags and baskets of food, casserole dishes, cake pans, salad bowls, and packages of buns and rolls. I held the door open as they filed into the house and went straight to the kitchen, where they quickly filled the table with all their dishes. Laughter and chatty banter flowed easily in the sunny space, a welcome energy after days of gloom and tears. The huge painting of Jesus with eyes that always followed us seemed to smile at the women from the wall above the microwave.

They scurried around, asking each other for ideas about how to lay out all the food. I stood in the corner watching and smiling, happy to be surrounded by all my favorite neighbor moms.

They fired off questions. *Can we use the microwave? What about the oven for the casseroles? Do you have an extra refrigerator or freezer?*

I easily answered their questions and directed them to various drawers for serving spoons and knives and any other dish they needed. I slid between all the bodies grabbing items from cabinets, and ducked underneath arms carrying plates and bowls of food. It felt like a game of Twister, all the women contorting as they moved and stretched here and there in our small kitchen.

"Do you know if your mom has napkins? We seem to have forgotten them."

I opened the wooden door off the kitchen into our bathroom and stepped up onto the bathtub to reach the high cabinet above the sink where we kept the napkins, paper towels, and extra toilet paper. I reached for the plastic package, relieved to find it full, and turned to hand it down to the neighbor mom.

"Wow. My daughter has no idea where most things are in the kitchen. You've been such a great help. Thank you so much."

The unexpected compliment threw me, and I nearly fell off the slippery tub like a wobbly gymnast on the balance beam. My heart swelled with pride.

I stepped down from the tub, unable to stop smiling as I followed her back to the kitchen to set up the buffet line. I happily cleared the table and set out the plates and napkins and silverware. I offered tips on how to set up the smorgasbord of food, having watched my mother assemble similar buffet lines for our family gatherings. We all worked together and hustled to get all the food laid out before the men arrived from the fields.

I walked over to the big dining room window as I heard the tractors coming back into the yard. Soon it looked like a farm implement dealer lot.

"They're coming," I announced as the men jumped down from their tractor seats and walked towards the house.

The screen door opened and the familiar faces of the neighbor men, husbands to the wives in the kitchen, dads to my friends, filed into the house, taking turns at the bathroom and kitchen sinks to wash their hands. Their booming voices and boots clopping along the floor created a symphony of baritones and bass drums. Our kitchen hadn't experienced this kind of life since we received the news.

They loaded their plates with food and filled in every chair around the dining room table, as well as the folding chairs and tables we had set up in the living room. They talked about farm equipment and the weather, and told stories about everything farmers normally talk about— late planting seasons, droughts, and hailstorms, the shared risks of farming. That day, they also talked about the shared task and commitment to one's own—a fellow farmer in need. The love and camaraderie in that room was palpable. These tough men loved each other, and this was the best way they knew to show it. And I loved them, for loving us.

When the meal was over, I stood proudly as the neighbors gathered their things and made their way to the door.

"You did a good job, kid."

"Thanks for all your help."

I blushed as many of the dads patted my head, with their calloused hands with dirt-stained fingernails as they filed past. The moms sidled up for half hugs or squeezed my shoulder as they loaded their cars and said their goodbyes. I watched as they drove away—a big smile on my face as I waved to the dust clouds as cars headed out in both directions. I walked back to the porch swing and sat down, smiling as I recalled their words. It was the first real joy that I'd experienced since that rainy day.

I was seen and appreciated; my worth so clearly measured by my helpfulness.

---

My helpfulness and farmgirl roots served me well in my professional roles. A couple months after I had accepted the job offer with the difficult boss, I stood nervously in line with my carry-on bag and faded green attaché case. The bag was 8 years old, having gone with me from college to my first job, through my graduate program and now to the world of state and national politics. I glanced around for my boss, but he was nowhere to be seen. Boarding had started, so I walked down the jetway onto the plane, taking my window seat and buckling up. Staring out the window, I imagined the next day and a half of meetings, and my stomach danced with excitement as I thought of the Arkansas capitol building and meeting the legislators and staff, whose names I'd rehearsed and memorized along with bill numbers and research statistics.

One of my first jobs was for a lobbyist, and I'd spent a great deal of time in Colorado's state capitol building. Blazers and business suits dominated the halls, and I had started padding my wardrobe with black pants and jackets. For this job, I purchased my first business suit, which was neatly folded in my suitcase. I'd worn it a few weeks prior for the big fall conference, and it became my uniform for any formal meeting. I loved the simplicity of basic black, and bought numerous shells of various colors to wear underneath.

The next day I followed my boss through the marble halls and up the dark wooden stairwell to the committee room. We listened to testimony and waited to hear an announcement concerning the bill on which my boss was to testify. The current topic proved to be quite controversial, and witnesses filled the chairs and dominated the afternoon's agenda. My boss knew a lot of people, and after the day's business concluded, we were invited to a lower-level office to discuss strategy. All my mental images of smoke-filled windowless rooms with men debating and ultimately agreeing and shaking hands were nearly fulfilled—minus the smoke. I was the only woman in the room and I listened quietly, but proudly, off to one side.

Relaxing on the hotel bed later that evening, I opened my journal and began to write. I noted the day's details, from meeting high-level state officials to drinking an afterhours glass of wine in the basement lounge lined with filing cabinets and pictures of historical figures and former policy leaders. I wrote that I had easily chatted with the agency director as well as with random citizens wanting to voice an opinion about politics. I had found common ground with the staffers and legislators from both parties.

*What a day*, I thought. I looked up and saw myself in the mirror across from me, my legs stretched out on the bed, my sleeveless periwinkle sweater showing off my lean arms. My jacket was draped over the chair, and my black leather boots sat on the floor below me. A big smile came across my face as I admired how good I looked, and how much I liked my suit. It looked good on me. The farmgirl had found a fancy replacement for her jeans and sweatshirts. The ornate capitol building and formal atmosphere was a far cry from those sweaty summer days spent in cornfields. My smalltown background allowed me to chat easily with the working man, while my time spent in bigger cities taught me the ropes of the white-collar world. I hadn't only found a wardrobe replacement, but a cozy fit for my intelligence and desire to affect change along with my ability to get along with any adults in the room. I saw clearly how I straddled both worlds—the simple farmgirl and the sophisticated state policy expert.

---

Working for my challenging boss included considerable managing, as I juggled my duties while filling in for my boss, completing the tasks that he hadn't done. I'd been on the job a few years before stepping into the de facto role as director. One employee was always designated as the go-to person when the boss was out of the office or simply not following through on his tasks. Some days I felt great about my role and ability to lead. My colleagues appreciated my responsiveness and thoughtful approach. Yet, on other days I resented the extra responsibility, knowing it didn't come with any real authority to make decisions.

"Where is the budget report for this project," the finance director asked, her eyes glaring at me, demanding an answer.

*Oh crap!* I thought. I didn't even know where to find the original budget or any current documents.

"I'm sure it's in his files. I'll find it and get it to you," I quickly stammered.

"I need it today! He said he'd send it to me yesterday. It was due last week, and I see he's not in the office, *again*." She complained, as she rolled her eyes, looking down the hall at his empty corner office.

"Ok. I'll get it to you this afternoon."

Panic rose in my chest and anger roiled in my belly. I couldn't believe he had missed yet another big deadline.

I searched his files, hoping to find the right folders to lead me to the budgets. I'd gotten better at recognizing his patterns and how he worked, but could never predict when he'd pad the budget with extra funds or wildly underestimate project costs. I wasn't sure if, when I'd be writing a report, I'd be begging for forgiveness, or asking for an extension.

I spent the rest of the afternoon in "boss" mode, channeling his thoughts and expectations, hoping I could complete the report in a way he'd approve and fulfill our finance department's needs. Most days included some interlude in his world, swapping my role for his. I took the criticism, rolling eyes, and frustrated rants from my colleagues as part of the job, and patted myself on the back for meeting everyone's needs.

Being outdoors counteracted the tension I'd felt when I had to play both of our roles—a rendition of Dr. Jekyll and Mr. Hyde that left me exhausted by Friday and dreading Monday. Thank God for the mountains, fresh air, and lack of cell service. Unplugging for two days helped. As my work responsibilities increased, however, so did my running and hiking miles.

At the start of 2013, only a few years into my de facto director role, I thought about my annual athletic goals and how I could manage work stress. I was in great physical shape, feeling stronger than I had in years, and with the constant work frustration I needed an equal amount of activity to balance it out. I decided to train for another marathon, so Alan and I decided to schedule our Utah vacation for the week after the race. I knew I could fit my long runs in the morning before biking to the office, and could sneak in workouts during my lunch hour. It felt satisfyingly good to arrive at work with everyone else in the mornings and take as much time for running at lunch as I would for a working lunch meeting. I could feel the buzz of my first hit of the runner's high coming to my rescue.

In the summer of 1985, just months after my sister's diagnosis, I sat on the edge of the second-floor barn door, overlooking the cement pad and metal pig feeders, my legs dangling above the snorting sows below me. No one could see me. The door was located in the back corner, hidden by the remaining hay stacks in the main barn area. The opening faced east towards the cornfield and abandoned farmhouse just over the hill. I came here to be alone with my emotions. I wanted to cry, but even the presence of the pigs stifled my tears. I couldn't cry in front of them.

So, I just sat and watched my feet swing back and forth, wondering what it would feel like to fall onto the cement below. Would I die? Or just break my leg? Maybe I would be fine, landing on my feet like a cat. I leaned into the frame and held onto the wood as I peered down at the ground. It didn't seem that far away. But it also looked too scary to jump. I scooted my butt back a few inches and tried to focus on the rows of corn in the distance. My heart thumped as flashing images blocked out the green field: the funeral home and the first wake I'd attended, with my friend Nichole hunched over in grief, barely able to lift her head. I imagined my sister in a casket. Me hunched over, buried in sorrow. Fear built up like a storm cloud, rising from the blue sky, billowing wider and higher into the sky until it blocked out the blue sky, turning a menacing gray. I felt like I could explode.

I stood up and dusted off the hay stuck to my shorts. I walked briskly out of the barn into the bright sunshine. I glanced over at our neat white farmhouse with its olive-green trim, but I kept on walking. I knew I should go inside, but I just couldn't. I walked along the gravel driveway and headed toward the road, not knowing where I was going but unable to stop my legs' momentum. I reached the end of our lawn and crossed over to the other side of the gravel road. I turned left, away from my best friend's house, and started walking down the stretch of road lined only by fields.

The narrow gravel road didn't have much of a shoulder, so I hugged the weedy ditch. My legs began moving faster and faster with each step taken. Soon I was on top of the knoll overlooking our neighbor's big white barn with the fields and strips of timber to the east. My knees lifted higher with each stride, and soon I was running down the other side and out of sight from our farm. My arms pumped, as sweat began to bead on my upper lip. I looked down at my navy cutoff sweats with the powder-blue pinstripes on the thighs and my worn-out white tennis shoes. Dust clung to my ankles and turned my white socks a rusty tan.

The road flattened, and I could see miles into the distance. Green fields of corn and alfalfa and two-story farmhouses lurked on the far-off ridge. Big puffy clouds dotted the summer blue sky, and I breathed in the smell of fresh-cut hay along with humid air. I rounded the corner, and passed the long lane leading to the stately white farmhouse with the wraparound porch, where a sweet old couple lived.

To my young mind, the distance felt immense, especially on my own two feet. The rolling fields and high ridge views looked so different from the ground. I'd been a passenger in cars, trucks, tractors—even on my bike—and had taken in this scene hundreds of times before, but never on foot. I was never this close, or moving this slowly, to witness the openness and experience just how far one could see from up here. And to discover just how infinitesimal I felt against this wide-open space, yet still feel connected and even comforted by its vastness. Soothed by the fresh air and endless horizon, I could make out the ski area across the river and a barn near the highway that, as a crow flies, wasn't far, but in a car meant taking two or three roads. I couldn't see our farm nor any of its outbuildings. I was out of sight and, for those few minutes and miles on the road, free from the reality that existed tucked on the other side of the small hill.

I kept on running. After another quarter mile, I stopped at the big metal mailbox that stood at the end of my friend's drive. I wanted desperately to run down and find Cindy. To tell her that I just ran to her house! And to escape into her world and play in the huge bedroom she shared with her sisters. Or to just sit in their garden and watch in awe and a little disgust as she ate tomatoes straight from the vine.

I stood on the side of the road a little out of breath; my hands clutching the ends of my shorts as I leaned over and rested on my knees. Sweat poured down my legs in rivulets of salty grime. I'd never seen my legs sweat like that before. I could feel the warm liquid rolling down my back and pooling in the chubby folds of my preteen belly. I pulled the neck of my baggy thrift shop t-shirt up and wiped my face, trying to sop up the stinging sweat dripping into my eyes. The streams of perspiration poured out my anxiety like refreshing rains being released from billowing storm clouds.

I looked around and could not see anyone or any man-made structures, except the dilapidated barn that sat with its bowed roof and graying boards behind a stand of trees to the north. I was just one mile from home, but worlds away in the safety of the undulating land around me.

I wanted to keep going, but I imagined my mother eventually discovering I was gone and wondering who might do the dishes. Or worse, her driving around in the car, only to find me by the ditch. Her long skinny index finger wagging at me, telling me to go home and for Pete's sake, not to run on the road with all this dust. You could get hit.

I reluctantly turned around and began jogging back to home. The gentle breeze dried my sticky bangs, enabling them to finally release their grip from my forehead. My ponytail slapped against the nape of my neck, its ends now matted with sweat. I watched red-winged black-birds swoop in front of me, with their splash of yellow feathers reflecting in the sunlight. I grabbed the bottom of my shirt's hem and wiped my upper lip, allowing the wind to blow across my stomach before quickly covering up my pale moist skin. I let my legs carry me forward and glanced down to watch them in action. Strong and tan, they didn't look like the same legs that I usually wished were longer and skinnier. The loose fabric of my shorts flapped against my thigh just above my knee, showing just enough of my quads to see the muscles flex with each step. My body moved with ease, practically floating along the dusty road. I could finally breathe. The anxiety and worry had been pounded into the limestone rocks beneath my feet. The fear and scenes of imagined caskets were no longer suffocating me.

I reached the neighbor's barn and sprinted up a small hill until I saw the top of our silver corn bin glinting in the sun, with the big red barn behind it. I walked the last 100 yards to our driveway. Each step slower and stride shorter, until I was taking baby steps into the yard. I sat down on our porch swing and wiped at the sweat and dirt on my face, using the remaining dry spots of my t-shirt. I took off my shoes and socks, revealing a distinct tan line of dirt on my ankles. Turning my sock inside out, I rubbed the dirt off my calves until my sock was as brown as the road. Leaning back, I let the swing rock back and forth as the salt dried on my face and legs. I closed my eyes and breathed deeply, in rhythm with the sway of the wooden bench.

On that day I found a salve for my wounds that no one could take away—a medicine stronger than even my favorite porch swing or barn loft window. The power of movement and physical exertion with the wind at my back and sun on my face; it was an exhilarating freedom. The liberation of being alone in my thoughts, surrounded by the life force of trees and plants growing in the fields. That simple activity of running transformed my isolation into a communion with nature, and helped me release the pressure of sadness that threatened to suffocate me. It flew away with the sunny summer breeze.

I looked up towards the road, still wondering how and why I decided to run down its dusty path. Shaking my head in both gratitude and wonder, I smiled at the magic I'd discovered on that unplanned journey. Sweaty and proud, I walked confidently into the house.

Running in the outdoors became my sacred space and where I went to make sense of the world. It was both therapy and an escape. The antidote to my pain and where I could go to feel whole and powerful.

---

On that day, I became a runner. I ran throughout my troubled teen years. I ran when I felt fat, or if some boy at school didn't like me. I ran when I felt ashamed of my hand-me-down clothes and free lunch tickets. I ran to clear my head and soothe my soul. I ran when things went wrong, and when I wanted to celebrate. I ran after getting accepted into my choice college. I ran when I was recruited to play college basketball. And I kept running through my 20s. I ran in Ecuador during my 9-month volunteer mission, usually the only gringa on the dirt streets of our dusty neighborhood. I even ran during a bout with giardia when my bowels could dump at any moment. And they did—more than once.

After I had returned to the States, a friend invited me to run a marathon with her as part of the Leukemia Society's Team-in-Training program. In all my years of running, I had only run one other race—an open cross-country 2.2 mile meet that my high school basket-ball coaches had encouraged me to run. Usually, all my running had been solo, with no set distance or pace.

I was nervous about agreeing to that marathon invi-tation, mostly because of my intestinal issues. Those anxieties were quickly dismissed by the challenge and excitement of pushing myself 26.2 miles for the very cause that had started my running obsession in the first place. It felt like one of the few tangible ways that I could honor my sister and her struggle. She survived two years of chemo; I could run 26.2 miles. And I did.

I continued running in my 30s, taking part in a few races every year. I ran during my lunch hour with co-workers, where I found a new way to enjoy running—with other runners. I tackled another marathon to see if I could beat my first time—my I-just-want-to-finish goal. I ended up shaving 15 minutes off my time.

I lived in 10 different places in 10 years. In each new city, I searched for apartments near running trails, whether it be a paved path through the city, a crushed gravel trail through trees, or a well-worn footpath down the middle of a tree-lined parkway in a posh neighbor-hood. Running was my outlet, my time to be outside and breathe in the peace of Mother Nature.

There was only one time in my life that I chose to cut back on my running—while I was working full time and attending graduate school. Even then I would sneak in a run on the weekends when I wasn't in class, but I tended to let my running shoes gather dust as I plowed through my coursework. Six months into my studies, I had that dark mole removed from the back of my leg that was diagnosed as melanoma. The surgery to fully remove the cancerous tumor and surrounding tissue left a scar across the entire back of my knee, right where it bends. I was on crutches for 3 weeks, and then walked with a limp for months. Running was definitely out of the question. Of course, it was the only thing I could think about as well. Although I had consciously chosen to cut back, the cancer scare changed everything. I needed to run. It was my salve, and my cancer was a big wound.

A month after surgery I tried running, fighting through the stabbing pains throbbing in the back of my knee, as the skin stretched and pulled with each stride. The sun was rising in the distance and despite the pain, I'd never felt better. I was going to be able to run again. It took six months before I could crank out my usual six-mile workout.

Running remained my escape, and in 2013 when I decided to run another marathon to counteract the stress of my demanding job and difficult boss, I set a goal to qualify for the Boston Marathon. Qualifying for Boston was the holy grail of road running—you have to be fast enough and meet specific time standards to even get into the race. I first learned of the status and honor of running in Boston during my first marathon, and I vowed to get there someday. Now 39 years old, I needed to run almost 30 minutes faster than my previous two marathons to meet the qualifying time. It was a big goal for me, having never run competitively. No track or cross country, and no formal coaching in the sport. But after the Leukemia

Society marathon, I was bitten by the Boston bug and started to dream of running in that iconic race. With all my work stress, it felt like a way to do something for me and to honor my upcoming 40th birthday.

---

I followed my training plan, feeling confident about my preparation, and eagerly anticipated race day and our Utah vacation. The run was on a Sunday morning, and Alan and I planned to leave for our vacation that afternoon. The familiar tune of my alarm woke me at two-thirty in the morning. It was pitch black and as much as I wanted to stay snuggled under the covers, I was anxious to get moving. My energy bar sat on the nightstand waiting to be eaten. I stealthily slid myself out from under the covers and into the bathroom where my race clothes were laid out. The deodorant ready to go. Vaseline for my toes, sunscreen for my legs. I looked at myself in the mirror and told myself that today was the day I would qualify for Boston. I could feel it in my bones. This run was for Carla.

I gathered my drop bag, kissed my boyfriend and beagle goodbye, and set out in darkness for the hour drive to a bus that would take runners up the canyon for the start of the race. As I made my way north, I saw the half-moon off to the east. It was beautiful and big, bright and inspiring. Some stars remained in the pre-dawn darkness. I thought of my cousin Carla, who died just two and a half months ago. She's up there somewhere. She's here with me. I could feel her presence and encouragement. A good omen, I thought. Today is going to be a beautiful clear day.

On the bus I found a nice window seat to curl up in and mentally prepare for the race. Nervous energy kept me from relaxing; I was so ready to start running. I had trained well for this race in what I found to be the best way for me. Not running constantly, but cross-training—hiking, biking, and running. I felt great—strong and fit. I was meeting my pace times on my long runs. I believed I could do it. I kept picturing the finish line, and imagining a 3:44:30 finish time. It would be just under the wire to meet the 3:45 qualifying time for Boston. I knew I wouldn't shatter that time; I just wanted to beat it. Heck, 3:44:59 would work for me. I just wanted the glory of crossing that finish line, knowing that I'd achieved a goal I had never thought possible.

A young woman sat down next to me on the bus, bringing my attention back to reality. We started with the usual pre-race questions: *Is this your first marathon? Have you run this course before?* When we got to the subject of time goals, we found we were both hoping to qualify for Boston. She was placed in a younger age bracket and would, therefore, have to run a lot faster. She had run a couple races before, and was close to her qualifying time.

"What do you do for a living?" I asked.

"I am working in the research field. I am hoping to get a PhD."

This girl is an overachiever, I thought to myself. But what would I expect from a marathoner? One must be a little Type A to tackle 26.2 miles in a Boston qualifying time.

She proceeded to tell me a little about her field of study, which included some work on melanoma. Although, she'd like to move to a different area.

"Really?" I responded. "I am a melanoma survivor. I was diagnosed nearly 12 years ago."

"Wow—that's great. It's a serious disease if it spreads."

"I know."

We chatted for the remainder of the bus ride and parted ways after arriving at the start line. She went to find her pace group, and I went off to find mine. I was filled with lots of emotions and thoughts as I recalled our conversation and my cancer survival status, my cousin's untimely death, and the fact I was standing in the 8:30 pace group hoping to run the fastest 26.2 miles of my life. All with stitches in my back from the mysterious lump biopsy.

The air was chilly as crowds of runners paced around, some running to stretch their legs, others like me, hopping around to keep fingers and toes from going numb. As the start time drew near, I kept visualizing myself crossing the finish line at that 3:45 qualifying time. I kept telling myself I could do this and to leave it all on the pavement. It was Boston or bust.

The starting gun sounded and as I hit the button on my Ironman watch, I could feel the months of training powering my legs down the canyon. The first 15 miles followed the winding road down the canyon and meandered along the river. The views were stunning and kept me distracted from the miles ahead. I saw the burn area from the recent wildfire that left behind charcoal stains on the trees and burned grass. I could see water bubbling as it flowed around the big creek boulders. I could hear birds singing and felt a gentle breeze on my face. It was a beautiful day.

As we neared the mouth of the canyon, spectators lined the road on both sides. They were all cheering and looking for their special someone trotting down the hill. I felt great and spotted my personal cheerleader running along the side of the road, clapping, and shouting my name, his camera hanging around his neck. I loved this man. I couldn't believe he gave up a gorgeous Sunday morning to fight a crowd of spectators and drive to the viewing spots along the route. He's my loyal supporter—and cute to boot.

Seeing Alan gave me an extra boost to push up the only minor hill on the course. Unfortunately, I was also feeling a boost from my bowels. I couldn't believe it. I was going to have to find a porta potty—soon! I was nearing the 18-mile aid station, where I knew there were restrooms as well as water and Gatorade. I was slightly ahead of my goal pace, so I hoped a quick trip to the lavatory wouldn't affect my time goal. Perhaps a freed colon would make me run faster.

I ducked into the first open porta potty and squatted over the top of the mountain-sized stack of toilet paper and human waste. I was in and out in less than 2 minutes. I took off and focused on gaining back those two minutes and reimagining a 3:44 finish. I would make it happen.

Mile 20 was the last time I saw Alan or any other spectators. The remaining route followed a cement bike path on the outskirts of town. I could feel my pace slowing, as my legs grew tired. I hadn't run a marathon in 8 years. I had forgotten how brutal those last 6 miles can be. I still felt pretty good, but I knew I was falling behind my time goal. I kept telling myself to push it—to do it for Carla.

I was talking to her in my head, trying to glean advice, inspiration, and most of all energy. I had one more energy chew in my waist belt and hoped it would give me the kick I needed. I put it in my mouth and forced myself to eat it, praying it would bestow magical powers into my legs.

As I rounded the bend into a forested trail area, I saw a woman jump into the pack. "Sixty more minutes of pain. That's all you have to do. Sixty minutes is nothing. You can sacrifice 60 minutes for the pride in knowing you will run in Boston."

She ran next to a young woman who clearly was on the same mission that I was that day. They both picked up the pace. I tried to keep up, but my legs just couldn't quite move that fast anymore. I played her mantra over in my head, while trying to believe I could inflict enough pain on myself in the next 60 minutes to stay on pace. At that point, I needed to run at a faster pace to make up for the minutes lost in the bathroom and my slowdown over the last mile or so. My mind really wanted to run, but my body was unable to respond.

I did the math in my head, and my calculations were clear. There would be no Boston. I had simply lost too much time. I was angry and disappointed. I kept cranking out the math in my head and tried to push my legs to go faster. I didn't want to believe what my calculations revealed. I felt so defeated—I had been so confident at the beginning of the race. I had trusted myself to overcome my own insecurities, yet here I was again, failing, missing the mark. What happened to my grand plan? All those training miles? It wasn't enough. I felt defeated in a way that surpassed how one should feel because of a race. It felt like something more.

My legs slowed with each agonizing step, and the weight of my failure was nearly unbearable. Runners were passing me, and I couldn't do anything to keep up with them. I had completely forgotten what the body does after 20 miles. The fatigue that sets in when your body runs out of fuel, and you hit the so-called "wall". I had run smack into it!

I calculated how slow my time was really going to be. Doing the math based on my current pace, I realized that I *could* potentially still finish in under 4 hours. I felt a surge of adrenaline and renewed pride as I settled into my revised goal. A sub-four-hours marathon isn't bad for this 39-year-old amateur runner. With each passing mile I redid the math, and my calculations still predicted a sub-four. I kept hoping that I could somehow manage to sprint to the finish and beat my Boston goal. But with each mile, it became clearer that the best I could do would be to finish in under 4 hours. I started feeling better about my effort and happy that I would shatter my previous marathon times by nearly 20 minutes, but my Boston Marathon goal would have to wait.

I rounded the last curve and headed into the home-stretch—the finish line banner was in sight. The clock and its red digital numbers ticked off the seconds: 3:51:39 and counting. My legs were turning into jelly, and the cramps were becoming unbearable. For the first time in my running life, my lungs felt as if they were going to collapse. I had a hard time catching my breath. I forced my legs to move faster, as I gave one final push. I stepped on the red-carpet finish line at 3:53, and shot my hands up in the air. I may not have qualified for the Boston Marathon, but I knew that I'd left everything on the pavement. I stumbled through the line as volunteers took my timing chip and placed a finisher's medal around my neck. I nearly threw up, as my legs began buckling. I thought I would collapse. Alan emerged out of the crowd with a huge smile plastered on his face. He grabbed and hugged me tight. I held on, fighting back tears and vomit. I leaned on his arm as we walked over to the after-party.

I was excited for my sub-four-hour finish, and my dreams of Boston floated easily away into the blue sky full of puffy clouds. I'd come close to my qualifying time goal, and knew that my slower finish wasn't just due to my bathroom break. I had easily reverted to my usual rationale that settles for "close enough". My subconscious motto had been to keep expectations low, so my fall was easier to accept. I shouldn't have been surprised that I didn't make it. I had merely hoped that Carla's spirit would somehow magically project me across the line in time. "Close" was my consolation, once again. I *almost* did it. I had *nearly* qualified. Just like my high school basketball team *almost* made it to the state tournament. I *almost* had a full ride scholarship to college.

I kept flashing back to my shortness of breath and near collapse at the end. I had never felt that kind of pressure in my chest. I hoped it was just pure exhaustion, but the image of the four women in white coats carefully excising the lump on my back returned to my mind. What if my pain and exhaustion wasn't merely from 26.2 miles, but something bad lurking within my seemingly healthy running body? I had a feeling my euphoria would be short-lived. I felt like I was walking on air, but an invisible weight was dragging me down from the clouds. I was ecstatic and terrified at the same time. I knew somewhere deep down that the real race was yet to come.

After grabbing some food, Alan and I decided to head back home. We wanted to get on the road for our Utah trip, and I was anxious to begin our vacation. As I walked to my car, I decided to call my mom. She was one of the few people who knew I was running the marathon, and I was proud to tell her of my personal record finish.

"This is so great, Rochelle. I am so happy for you, and so glad life is so good for you."

A hot rush of fear flooded my veins and flushed my cheeks.

"Yes, life is good," I replied.

The knot, however, tightened in my stomach. I felt so bad for her; I knew this high wasn't going to last.

*three*

—

# Seeing the Bottom

T hree months before my failed bid to qualify for the Boston Marathon, I sat in the back row as the funeral home director carried in a small wooden podium and set up more chairs around me. My parents, sisters, and I sat in a row. I was at the end, with my older sister Jolene to my left. My aunts, uncles, and other family members filled the chairs in front of me.

My cousin Carla was two years younger than Jolene, and two years older than me. We were very close growing up, and her sudden death had hit us hard. Jolene and I walked together through the viewing line and cried as we kneeled before the casket. As we stood up, my uncle glanced at us and began crying even harder.

"And we thought we would lose you," he sobbed, pulling Jolene into a bear hug.

Tears pooled in my eyes and my throat burned, as I watched the two embrace and acknowledge the truth of his words. I was crying for him, for Carla, and for the gift of Jolene.

My sister and I hugged Carla's mom, our cousins, and their spouses. We walked through the funeral home looking at all the posted pictures and memories associated with the images. "I remember that shirt," I said, pointing to one of her middle-school pictures. We smiled and cried some more, looking over photos of us and our families.

"I still can't believe it," Jolene somberly stated, glancing towards Carla's casket.

"I know."

We found a place to sit, and then watched as friends and family stood or kneeled before Carla's casket and shared tender moments with her parents and siblings. It broke my heart wide open.

"Who's that?" I whispered to Jolene as I pointed towards a stranger. "Do you remember that woman?"

"I think she was at graduation parties, but I don't remember her name."

I nodded, trying to remember my cousin Carla's graduation party from 20 years back. It would have occurred 2 years before mine. Were my aunt and uncle still living at their house with the grape vines growing on a trestle above the driveway? It was like a natural jungle carport, with green vines so thick that you could hardly see the wood to which they were clinging. Those vines also served as an umbrella, sheltering the graduation party-goers from the rain as we gathered around picnic tables beneath their verdant canopy. I could taste the chocolate pudding whipped cream dessert that my aunt always made. There had been so many parties on that driveway under the vines.

The priest whispered to others to take their seats, as he walked over to my uncle standing closest to the casket, motioning for him, my aunt, and cousins to take their places in the front row. I watched my uncle hobble to his chair, his gait off-kilter after his hip replacement, not knowing if the grimace on his face was from his physical pain or sheer grief. My cousins followed, with their heads bowed and hands clasped tightly in front of them. My heart shattered again, as I imagined the sudden and incomprehensible loss of their sister. I rested my chin on my chest, unable to face their sadness.

The hum of conversation finally subsided, and it felt as if a gust of heavy air filled the room with a palpable sadness as we remembered why we had gathered on this cold January night. No longer hidden behind the flow of visitors, my beautiful cousin Carla was lying in the casket at the front of the room.

The priest expressed his sympathy to all of us quietly seated in the folding chairs, each clutching onto our own memories in our own space. Many bowed their heads and grabbed the hand of a loved one next to them. I reached out for my sister's hand and held on tight. I couldn't believe we were sitting there while Carla was lying in the casket, wearing the same red sweater that we had seen her wearing just weeks before.

Three days before my cousin's funeral, I stood at the sink behind a sleek granite counter with funky fire red light fixtures overhead, gazing at the reflection of the television on the opposite wall. I half listened to the news while making dinner. Junior, my beagle, was sitting on the rug at my feet, waiting for me to drop something despite the fact I had just fed him. I was still chilled from our walk and grateful to be out of the cold dark January night.

My phone rang, and I saw on the screen that it was my cousin Carissa who lived nearby.

"Carissa, how are you?" I answered.

"Hey Rochelle, are you home?" her voice shook.

I hesitated slightly. "Yes, I am."

"Um, can I stop by? I'm only a few minutes away."

"Uh . . . sure." I replied, knowing something was wrong.

I stopped chopping and began pacing back and forth to the front door. Junior followed my every move, gazing up at me with his big brown eyes. I bent down, grabbed his floppy ears with my hands, and whispered, *I hope everything is OK.* He leaned his head against my leg.

The motion light flicked on, and I heard Carissa's footsteps on the sidewalk leading to my house. I opened the door before she could knock or ring the doorbell. My normally bubbly blonde cousin stood under the porch light, her head tilted to the side, her lips pressed together in a forced half smile, her blue eyes staring sadly right at mine. I gestured her inside, as I searched her eyes for answers.

She entered my house, then said, "We should sit down. I have bad news."

I stepped back and she entered and sat on the end of the couch along the wall. I stumbled over to the ottoman on the opposite corner, and sat down facing her. Junior jumped up beside her and put his paw on her arm, his customary request for some love. She stroked his head and cooed at him, as he nuzzled into her side.

She looked up and said, "It's Carla. She died today."

The words felt like cold icy air, as they stung and took my breath away. I stared into my cousin's crystal blue eyes, reaching out to pet Junior, simply needing to touch something to steady my hand.

"What? How can that be? What happened? We just saw her two weeks ago at Christmas."

I gazed out the window, remembering Carla's bright-red sweater she wore, as she had sat across from me in our aunt's basement, excitedly describing her plans for the new year. There had been a twinkle in her eye and ease in her voice that I hadn't seen or heard her have in a long time. I shared her excitement, as we envisioned her new goals. I imagined her thinner and happier, and less stressed.

I felt a wave of anger and sorrow rise within me as I realized that those images would never become reality. How unfair! She gave her heart and soul to the world, working with vulnerable populations and helping so many young people. It felt like another of life's ironies that she died when she was beginning to take better care of herself. It saddened me to think she would never get a chance to make those dreams come true.

---

I heard nothing that the priest said, or the bible passages he recited. My mind only saw flashes of us as kids. Carla's deep laugh; the way she spoke. Grandma's yard where we played softball. The track meet at my college when I watched her compete for the first time. Her picture in the local paper describing her athletic feats and national level competition. Our conversations about social injustices and our respective work in this field. Her coworkers phoning the authorities to perform a wellness check on her. The police finding her alone, dead in her home.

I then imagined cops breaking down my door, only to find me dead and alone.

The priest then welcomed family members to share whatever was in their hearts and nodded to one of her siblings as an invite to come forward. One by one, they stood before the rows of family and friends and spoke of their childhood, their relationships with their oldest sister, and the role she played in their family. How she took care of them. She was the glue in their family. They described her love of national parks and of the sibling trips they took, and of course, the bickering that occurs on family road adventures. Their love and adoration for their older sister was so apparent, along with their grief and uncertainty about how they would get along without her. I recognized some memories, but other stories and experiences revealed a deeper connection and bond among the siblings that I had not easily seen.

As each of my cousins shared memories of Carla, I felt myself sinking further down into my chair. I had thought that I might read the poem I had written, but instead my mind was filled with self-pity and loathing as I imagined my siblings gathered at my funeral. Not all of them would tell such heartwarming tales of sisterly love or caretaking. I imagined some of them squirming in their seats, checking their watches, wondering when they could leave and move on. Praying that the priest didn't invite them to say anything. Or worse, them telling all their stories about me as the mean older sister.

Jolene looked at me, her eyes asking if I was going to read my poem. I shook my head and looked downward at my hands, now firmly clasped together in attempt to hold in my grief and shame as they swallowed me whole.

———

Carla's death made me imagine my own funeral. What if I died suddenly? Who would show up, and what would they say? I shuddered to think about who would be seated in the pews for my own service. I had spent most of my time working, and those relationship connections were mostly superficial. Alan and I were growing closer, but we were only spending time together on the weekends. Would I even want a burial in my hometown? I hadn't lived in Iowa for nearly 20 years. I didn't even attend a church in Denver.

Returning to Colorado the day after Carla's funeral, I sat in the window seat of a regional jet, staring at the frozen brown fields sprawling out from the airport runway. My homeland—the rolling hills of eastern Iowa—were covered in crusty white snow. Puffs of exhaust hung in the frigid air as the plane revved to life. All the memories of Carla's death played like a never-ending film reel in my head, with images of cops and broken doors, my sobbing uncle and cousins, all the photos and newspaper clippings capturing her life and many accomplishments.

The final scene I imagined was me in a casket, with no one seated in the church pews. The similarities between Carla and I as single women, both working in social services and public policy, made me fear my own possible tragic death. Yet instead of endearing stories being told about me, I imagined only mumbles and whispers.

That image haunted my every thought. I reached down toward my carry-on bag, and pulled out the small spiral notebook with DO WHAT U LOVE TO DO printed on the front cover in pastel rainbow colors. Removing the turquoise pen that was tucked in the notebook's metal binding, I wrote, "Flying back from Carla's funeral . . . what an emotional roller coaster." I recounted my total stupor and uncontrollable sobbing when the news sank in, and my robotic motions at work preparing for bereavement leave away from the office. I remembered I was hiking when my cousin called to ask if I would read at the funeral mass.

I *needed* to write it down; get it out of my head. Document the moments—the emotions, laughter, and tears. To somehow capture those emotional days, realizing that I'd forget the details. The small things like the short but profound conversations I'd had with my family. Carla's death was the first death in our immediate family other than my grandparents. And she was only two years older than me.

I couldn't stop imagining my own death. I lived alone. I could die, and the first people to notice would be my coworkers who saw me the most often. Alan would notice next. Yet, my fingers couldn't write about my own funeral, even though I envisioned it so clearly in my mind. Me, lying in a casket in my hometown's funeral home.

My parents standing next to the casket, with my siblings milling around. Not many people were waiting in line to pay respect to my dead body. Few would miss me. A life that never really existed—one that only existed on weekdays. I'd been trying harder to make more friends; my hiking group was great. Meeting Alan was a major breakthrough. But the walls I'd so carefully built to protect my heart had also kept so many others out.

My throat tightened and I pressed my head against the plane window, a spider web of frost spun across the glass. I hoped that the cold would halt the tears burning under my eyelids. The sky was pitch black, so I looked hard toward the ground, searching for any light or distraction. Tears rolled down my cheeks, and my shoulders shook. I fumbled through my pockets, hoping to find a leftover funeral tissue stuffed inside. I turned my body and tucked myself in as close to the window as I could, thankful for the engine of the small plane that drowned out my whimpering sobs as I relived my adolescence.

Life had changed in our family after Jolene got sick. I had taken on more responsibilities to help my parents as they focused on my sister. While enjoying their praise for my good deeds, I also grew angry about my role as babysitter and resented my younger sisters, who from my vantage point, seemed oblivious to the challenges our family faced. I was barely a teenager, and they were 5 and 8 years old; I was constantly yelling at them to pick up their toys or to go outside and play. I called them names and bossed them around. Anger became the primary emotion that I could express, and they took the brunt of it.

My baby sister was born just before I entered high school. The additional sibling to care for ratcheted up my anger and resentment. I took part in a screaming match with the next oldest in the kitchen, and a shitstorm on the driveway when I lit into my younger sister for being disrespectful to our parents. My feelings had nowhere to go, and I knew no other way to deal with them other than lashing out. Looking back, I now can see clearly that I had suppressed my pain and sadness on the day when I'd read the note about Jolene's sickness straining to keep my fear to myself. But those feelings never went away, and I ultimately expressed myself with angry outbursts. Anger felt more acceptable than crying.

In my 20s, I sought counseling. I could finally see my feelings for what they were, and could understand and empathize with my younger self. Yet, I never shared those insights with my younger sisters, fearing that I'd only dredge up the past. I realized it was time to acknowledge my actions and apologize for taking my anger out on my sisters who had done nothing to deserve my wrath when we were kids.

As the plane took off, my thoughts drifted to my brother. My head dropped, and I let out an intense sigh. In college, I had written him an awful letter, freighted with my anger against men and blaming him for my disordered eating patterns, believing that some minor childhood indiscretions of his contributed to my body issues. However, I had forgotten that one horrible night at that high school party.

I had started drinking in high school. A good buzz seemed to release some of the pressure I was experiencing.

One night I drank too much, and a male friend offered to drive me home. He had a girlfriend, so I accepted his offer as a gentlemanly gesture and went along. When he began forcing himself on me I resisted then froze, unable to say no, protest, or stop his unwanted advances. Instead, I blamed myself and cursed my body. When that horrid memory resurfaced in my 30s, my disordered eating and body issues finally made sense. I binged on food to numb the pain and punish my body. My guilt over blaming my brother for my eating issues was profound. Yet, I was unable to tell him about that night, and the guilt and shame I associated with it. It was time. My brother needed to know the full story. I needed to ask for his forgiveness and express my true feelings for him, my only brother. The big brother who I admired, respected, and loved. I felt terrible for blaming him for something that someone else's actions had caused.

The sexual assault overwhelmed me, and I protected myself by suppressing my feelings that were too powerful to process. I felt violated and betrayed. I couldn't handle the fear of losing my sister to her illness. I didn't know how to process what felt like a violation of my very being. Instead, I shut down. It was the only way I knew how to still function—by not feeling anything at all.

I had spent my adulthood running from that very angry and ashamed girl. I learned to avoid my emotions and keep people at a distance. I had learned that helping others made me feel seen and appreciated, just like that spring planting day back on our farm with all the neighboring farmer wives. I realized that I could obtain human connection without revealing too much of myself. Pleasing bosses and bending over backwards in my job became my way of securing approval. Now I realized that keeping people at a safe distance would mean dying alone, with only my coworkers discerning my absence. I'd started making friends and opening up to Alan, but I still lived my life guarded. I needed to find a way to ask for forgiveness from my brother and sisters—and from myself.

I covered my face with my hands and leaned against the plane seat in front of me, my forehead pressed against the blue leather. Snot and tears trickled down together in my palms. I cried until nothing was left, blowing the mucous salty mess into my soaked tissue, wiping my eyes with the back of my hand.

"Flight attendants, please prepare for landing," the pilot announced.

I leaned my head back and closed my eyes, hoping that my red cheeks and bloodshot eyes would clear in the 20 minutes before we'd descend at the Denver airport. I deeply sighed, imagining the words that I needed to say to my sisters and brother.

A few weeks after the funeral, I sat at my desk and began drafting my apology letters to my sisters and brother. *I don't know how to start this . . . of course, major life events, especially death, bring up emotions one doesn't foresee coming. I guess I have a few things I want to say before I go to my grave . . . .*

I scribbled the letters into my journal, searching for the right words—the true message and intent of what

I hoped would flow through the combination of sentences on the paper. I apologized for having been a mean and angry sister—really, not being a sister at all. The exhaustive caregiving responsibilities I had assumed had made me feel more like a substitute mom than a sister. I had tried to help my parents as best I could, but I was just terrible at whatever role I seemed to play during their developmental years.

My attempts to control my life and abandon my painful memories of childhood was my one-way route out of my hometown. Many in our community went to college in nearby towns, then returned to raise their families. The subtle message was to stay close to home. However, I wanted nothing more than to leave and start over. To attend college and live on my own. Get a good job, use my brain, and leave all the heartache and bad memories behind. I was determined to stay single, definitely *not* have children, and experience the world.

I had judged my sisters for choosing different paths, and made it obvious that I'd thought their choices were unwise. I couldn't understand why they didn't want to flee our small town. I acted like a Catholic nun, swatting their wrists with rulers and condemning their wrong actions.

As I reflected on those self-righteous years, I felt lucky that my siblings even still acknowledged me. We weren't best friends who spoke every day, yet they still welcomed me into their lives when the family gathered. For that, I was extremely grateful. They had grown up to be amazing, strong women, despite my nagging, finger-wagging, and nasty name-calling.

My tears flowed freely as I transcribed my journal notes onto note cards and penned my apologies. I closed with a final *I am truly sorry* atonement to them. I folded the cards and addressed the envelopes. Taking a deep breath, I lifted the first envelope to my lips to seal it and paused. I closed my eyes and heard a faint whisper of hesitation in my head. But I took the flap and ran my tongue along the sticky edge, sealing each envelope shut.

Pushing my chair back from the big oak desk, I leaned back into the chair and placed my arms on the armrests. My heart raced as I tried to calm my breathing. *Breathe it in,* I told myself. *Breathe in the pain.* Isn't that what my favorite Buddhist nun Pema Chodron would say? *Breathe in the black nasty suffering and breathe out compassion and forgiveness.*

I thought I'd suffocate in my own darkness. I kept breathing, though, and knew I *needed* to send the letters. I *needed* to make peace with my past, to acknowledge what I had done and why, in order move forward. I didn't want to risk dying with all these feelings of guilt and sorry left unsaid. *What if I am the next Carla?*

I dropped the envelopes into the outgoing mail pile at work the next day.

———

After Carla died and I had sent my letters to my siblings, I felt a tug to become more involved in family events. Three months later, my mom would be retiring and my dad celebrating a milestone birthday. My family was throwing a party, and I realized that I had to attend— I needed to be with them. Usually I only returned to

Iowa for holidays and other major occasions, making at least one annual trip but not much more. I wished that I had been better about taking the time and spending the money to go back home, but I didn't visit regularly. I had missed birthdays, anniversaries, baptisms, first communions, confirmations, and graduations. And I certainly missed any of those spontaneous weekend get-togethers when my siblings, cousins, aunts, and uncles would gather at the farm for whatever reason.

I had run away from that familial closeness years ago, never feeling that I truly fit there. I had been burdened by my mistakes. Yet, sending those apology letters freed something inside me and finally allowed me to be real. I no longer carried the baggage of my past, no longer was I walking around a fretting mess, wishing I could apologize. Wishing I could tell them how terrible I felt. Wishing they knew how much guilt I carried for all the pain I'd caused them. With that burden gone, I could live freely. The secret was out. My burden was gone. The apology had been spoken and was no longer held in my head unexpressed.

Three months later, Alan and I attended the family party at the local restaurant back home. The celebration was important to me. My parents had sacrificed a lot through the years, and it felt good to honor them. The mood was jovial; everyone loves my parents. I made a point to stop at every table and laughed and joked with all my relatives. My brother couldn't make it, but all my sisters were in attendance. Nothing was said about my letters, but I felt an ease around my sisters that hadn't existed before.

I couldn't put my finger on the surge of sentimentality I felt, however, as I hugged my uncle. When he inquired when he might see us again I flinched, stating that I wasn't sure. It was partly due to my regret for not having been around more often, and my eerie feeling that I might never be back.

As we drove away from the party, I experienced an overwhelming sense of love and connection. Having sent my letters of apology to my siblings, I could finally just be with my family and feel like I belonged. I no longer carried my 1,000-pound weight of guilt for my failures as a sister.

Driving up and over the hill on the highway that I'd driven so many times before, I observed, for the first time in a long time, the beauty of that early spring hillside with its brown fading into green—new life starting to sprout and rise from the ground.

*four*
___

# Free Falling

A few days before leaving for my trip to Iowa for the family party, I stood in front of the mirror, brushing my teeth, and wearing my favorite rose-colored button-down shirt with a herringbone pattern. The perfect blend of business and feminine. My simple fake diamond necklace was neatly framed in the shirt's V-shaped neck. As I admired my visage in my favorite outfit, I noticed a little purple mark just above the sparkling gem, right on my collarbone.

It looked like a cross between a scratch and a bruise, and it seemed a wee puffy. I wondered what it was, assuming it was from those branches that swung back into my face on our hike up to Blue Mountain in Golden Gate Canyon. I didn't recall being hit with any of the scrub oak or pine branches, but being hit was the most logical culprit. I couldn't think of any other reason for a bruise to appear on my collarbone.

A week later, I met Alan after work for our usual out-and-back hike to the radio tower atop a prominent foothill on the city's edge. These short hikes were a perfect antidote to a stressful day, where I could pound out my day's frustrations through my boots.

The sky was dark when I pulled into my garage that evening. I had to wake up Junior, who was curled up in the car's back seat, exhausted from our hike. Entering the house, I dropped my backpack on the table in the kitchen and stepped into the bathroom to change into my pajamas. As I tugged at my sports bra and wrangled it over my head, I caught a glimpse of something ominous on my side. I turned to take a closer look in the mirror and saw a lump protruding from my rib cage. It wasn't bruised or discolored but looked like a glob of something lumpy stuck under my skin.

I quickly scanned my side and began feeling up alongside my breast where I felt another lump. On the top side of my right breast—an obvious lump. *Oh my god! It must be breast cancer!*

But the lump on my ribs didn't make sense. My mind raced as I tried to induce a logical reason for the appearance of these sudden lumps under my skin.

I placed my finger on the neck nodule that I had recently discovered the week before and wondered if they were connected. I had thought it was a bruise, but it persisted. It did not turn green and yellow like most bruises as they healed. I couldn't comprehend what could cause all the lumps to appear in such random and seemingly disconnected parts of my body.

I walked topless into my kitchen to grab my phone and call Alan.

"Hey—I have a lump on my ribs and my boob."

"What? What are you talking about?"

"I took my shirt off, and they were just there. One's on my rib and another on my right boob. I have no idea what to think. What the hell are they?"

He tried to calm me as he offered up possible reasons. Far-off possibilities like allergies or maybe even some weird bug bite. I couldn't voice any of my own guesses, not wanting to worry either of us. He had enough on his plate. I told him that I would call the doctor in the morning and not to worry about it.

That night I lay in my bed, staring at the ceiling fan, as fear filled the room. I could do nothing to stop it. The silence carried my thoughts and worries that smothered me. I tried pushing them aside, placing my hands up to my face to create a barrier between me and the heavy weight of fear crushing me. I rolled over and grabbed my journal from the nightstand. A short entry: *I am scared. Please don't let it be breast cancer. Oh please! Please! Please!* Jotting the words on paper made it real, but also made the weight of it more than my own. The little notebook now held some of my anxiety.

The lumps showed up in April, the same month as my employer's large company conference. The summer months were always packed with meetings and lots of business travel. My marathon and our Utah vacation was less than a week away.

The sun streamed through my office as I started my computer and opened my inbox. I placed my right hand on my collarbone and felt the little lump protruding as it had been for the last two weeks. Closing my eyes, I ran my left hand along my side, where a similar bump greeted me on my rib. I sighed deeply. As much as I wanted to start typing email responses and focus on work, I knew I had to make that call to my doctor.

I closed my office door, removed the insurance card from my wallet, and dialed my doctor's number. The automated answering system gave me the option of speaking to a nurse. I pressed the number on the keypad, waiting for someone to answer and tell me it was nothing. I explained the lumps to the nurse who answered my call. She wasn't sure what the lumps would be, given their varied locations and appearances. The one on my neck had a purplish tint, while the others had no discoloration. She asked if I had any allergies, infections, used new laundry detergents, or made other changes to my routine. I could find no easy source to blame.

She wanted to help, but finally convinced me that I needed more than a phone consultation. "I think it would be best to see a doctor so they can make a determination."

She connected me to the doctor's scheduler, and I made an appointment for the next day to see my primary care physician.

That evening two more lumps appeared, this time on my back. I kept trying to brush them off as something simple. Perhaps a virus, or a weird infection. Yet, my gut never fully believed in these simplistic answers. I knew something was wrong—very wrong.

---

"It's not melanoma," my primary care physician told me after he carefully examined the lumps. "I don't know what it is, but let me ask some of my colleagues if they have any ideas."

He left the room, and I breathed a sigh of relief that it wasn't melanoma. That hadn't even crossed my mind. Breast cancer was my only concern. But given my history, I knew that melanoma was always part of the equation.

"The other doctors didn't have any other ideas either. To be safe, let's do a biopsy and go from there. I will put in an order. They will call you to schedule an appointment." With that, I walked out and returned to work.

Within 3 hours, the surgical department called me. They wanted me to come in ASAP. Would 3 p.m. work?

Suddenly, a hot choking sensation filled my throat as my stomach began churning. I knew that doctors rushed nothing *unless it needed to be rushed*. My first melanoma excision had been scheduled for two weeks out, despite my anxious pleas to schedule it quicker. At that time, the doctor assured me it was okay to wait. I got the message loud and clear. What might feel like life or death to a patient may just be a routine case to a doctor who sees hundreds of cases annually. Doctors are better equipped to judge life or death, and they know that to manage their workloads they must allocate their precious resources accordingly. It's triage at its purest form.

My fear as I waited in the surgical department's waiting area was palpable. I could taste it. See it. Hear it. Touch it. Like a freight train barreling down on me, the noise of my anxiety grew louder with each passing second. But I kept fighting it off. I kept telling myself, *It's going to be OK. I can't be that sick! The marathon is in five days' time, and I'm in the best shape of my life.* My only problem was exhaustion. But I chalked that up to marathon training. I cycled through the signs of cancer that used to be posted off our family's bathroom medicine cabinet, left over from my sister's leukemia diagnosis. *Fever—no; diarrhea—no; weight loss—no* (dammit); *loss of appetite—no* (I was eating like a pig.) Nothing lined up, other than exhaustion.

A nurse called out my name and escorted me to the surgical room where they'd perform the biopsy. She instructed me to take off my shirt and bra and put the gown on, leaving it open in the back. She left the room, and I did as I was instructed and waited. My hands were tightly clasped in my lap, as I stared at the surgical suite's white walls and table, the metal cabinets along the walls, in addition to boxes of gloves and medical equipment. The room was large, however I felt miniscule in my little chair against the wall.

Soon the door opened and in walked four women in white coats. My skin pricked up like a dog's fur rising on its back, and I immediately sensed danger. My puny lumps *surely* did not require four people to remove them. They were the size of peas.

The surgeon shook my hand, then introduced herself and her entourage. She explained they were residents, and taking part in my biopsy was part of their training. I tried to believe her, but I felt like a lab rat waiting to be dissected, analyzed, and left for dead.

We talked about the lumps, how long I'd had them, where they started. When did I have my first melanoma? Where was it? Did I have any other moles?

I couldn't figure out why they kept asking about my melanoma. The doctor told me it wasn't that.

"Any symptoms? Have you lost weight?"

No—much to my chagrin. I wanted to be five pounds lighter for the race. They all listened intently with straight faces. She looked over my lumps and was trying to figure out which one to biopsy.

"They're all pretty small," she said.

"I know. I assume you'll be digging them out and I'll need stitches?"

"Yes. It should just be a couple sutures. I think the ones on your back might be the best ones to biopsy." She felt the one on my rib cage, and then the one in the middle of my back.

"Can you do me a favor?" I asked. "I'm running a marathon on Sunday. I'd prefer if the stitches weren't going to be rubbed by my sports bra."

"Oh, sure," the surgeon replied. "About where does your sports bra hit? I think this one," feeling the lump that was in the middle but lower on my back, "should give enough clearance. And it should be fairly healed by Sunday. I don't think it will be a problem."

"That sounds great. I've had many moles removed and I know the most pain will be tomorrow and the day after. Thanks."

"Yes, you're right." She numbed the area, and soon was taking a little slice out of my back. "This is really small and soft, but I think I can get the whole thing," her voice straining slightly as I could tell she was trying so very hard to remove the foreign object in one piece.

"I got it," she declared triumphantly.

"Can I see it?" I said, genuinely excited and interested to see what kind of alien was lurking beneath my skin.

"Sure." She held out her hand with the little white globule resting comfortably in her palm. It looked like a big ball of tapioca. It looked harmless enough. And her calm demeanor relaxed me a bit.

One of the residents stitched me up as the surgeon gave them little pointers on how to thread the material to provide the most coverage and least pinch. I got dressed as the surgeon finished up her notes.

"The results should be in by Thursday but I am going out of town, so I won't get the results to you until next week when I'm back in town."

"That's fine," I said. "I'm going on vacation after the marathon, so if I'm dying don't call me," I half-laughingly commented.

"Oh, I'll get the results to you as soon as possible. Good luck on your marathon."

Alan met me in the lobby, and we walked to a nearby bar to have a drink and eat. I tried to casually explain the process, the jokes about sports bras and how kind the surgeon was to biopsy the one furthest from my bra line. He listened and tried to laugh at the female humor, but we both knew it was all fake. I was trying to be calm for him and he for me. Deep down, I knew the situation was very bad. The urgency with which the biopsy was scheduled. The four medical professionals. The barrage of questions about my previous melanoma. Alan, I think, sensed the same. We drank our beer, choked down some food, and headed back to our cars.

"Do you want me to come to your place?" he inquired.

I hesitated. I didn't want to be needy but responded, "Yes, that might be good. I'll need someone to help me put on a clean bandage in the morning. I don't think I can reach it on my own."

"I can do that for you," he replied, with a sympathetic smile.

We walked to our cars and headed to my house. I think we both knew it had nothing to do with bandages, but our mutual need to just be together, even if only to hold our fears in silence. It was the holding that was necessary. I spent the night curled up in his arms, silently praying all of this would go away.

———

The surgeon was right; the incision healed quickly and didn't bother me during the race. I tried to forget the marathon, my failure to qualify for Boston and push aside any thoughts of biopsies and doctors as we headed west. Excitement, anxiety, and plenty of sore muscles rode along with me as we drove across Colorado after the marathon. Our first vacation.

The pine forests and mountains flattened into high desert mesas and flat expanses of sagebrush and dusty dirt. The sky widened the further west we drove, until we could see for miles. The silhouettes of rocky buttes created shadows on the horizon. We were finally in Utah, and it looked like we had arrived on a surreal red rock planet. I stared out the window at the massive swells of sandstone and flat stretches of arid ground.

We passed the turnoff to Moab and entered a new-to-me stretch of highway. The scenery was so different from our Colorado alpine environment but no less stunning. I loved seeing new places. I preferred loop hikes rather than out-and-back routes. I always tried to never run the same race twice. And I loved to travel and experience new places and people. Utah had intrigued me from the first pictures I saw of Bryce and Zion as a teenager to my first backpacking trip a few years prior. The red rocks and unnatural landscape fascinated me. From a distance, it appears lifeless with all the stone, but up close you can see little berries on the juniper trees, the flowers jutting out of tiny cracks, and plenty of tiny lizards scurrying about the sand and rocks.

We turned off the interstate, choosing the scenic route to our destination. We weren't in a hurry, and we wanted to see as much as we could during our 8-day adventure. First stop was Capitol Reef National Park.

Heavy clouds hung in the sky as we pulled into the visitor center's parking lot. It was a good thing that we'd just planned to drive through the park—there would be no hiking for my sore legs just yet. We picked up a map and decided to cruise the 8-mile Scenic Drive.

The road weaved through a series of orchards, the perfect rows of green trees a stark contrast to the wall of red towering over the oasis of fruit trees. It looked unnatural amid the harsh rock and vertical cliffs. The pavement narrowed and crossed over swaths of sandy arroyos; road signs warned of high water during rains. It was easy to see how these little ditches could fill and overtake the road as it dipped down along the depression's contours. It was sprinkling lightly, and I hoped it wouldn't start raining much harder as we made our way back to the heart of the park.

A huge wall of rusty red jutted nearly straight up from the shrub-dotted ground. Its color and texture made me think of an enormous chocolate block, with big chunks chiseled out of its hulking sides. I'd never seen rock that color or such clean-cut lines. It was easy to imagine the rock splitting at some point, but where did the pieces go? There was no obvious evidence of rock chunks lying on the ground below. I stared at the walls, studying the angular edges, as I imagined tasting bittersweet chocolate in my mouth while we drove along.

We stopped to take pictures from the car, not wanting to step out into the drizzle and clouds. My legs were content to remain still; I had hoped they would feel better before our hike the next day.

"We'll have to return and go hiking," Alan said.

"Wouldn't it be cool to walk along those walls? They look like chocolate blocks."

He laughed, agreeing with my metaphor. Alan was getting used to my imagination and all the crazy things I "saw" on our hikes or just driving about in the car. My active imagination of human faces and animal bodies. It must hark back to my childhood days staring up at the clouds, competing with my brother for the most unusual or creative name for the billowing white shapes lazily lingering above our heads.

We took our time driving, noting trail signs and making mental notes of the park's layout and the narrow four-wheel-drive track slicing through the towering walls, wishing we had a vehicle capable of exploring its windy path. Reaching the end of the scenic drive, we stopped and took in the amazing formations as I wondered aloud how these massive rocks came to be, and how Mother Nature could create such unique shapes and colors. We were in a kaleidoscope of the entire orange to red spectrum.

We mumbled lots of "wows" and "oh my gosh," plenty of "look at that" or "my goodness it's so beautiful." This drive was already worth the 8 hours and price of a national parks pass.

Driving south on Highway 12, we gradually gained elevation, and the landscape turned from red to forest green as we entered Dixie National Forest. It felt like Colorado with its tall pines and white-barked aspens. *This would be beautiful in the fall*, I thought. *Another place to come back and explore.* The hilltop views spread out for miles, and we commented on the variety of landscapes that we'd passed through since crossing the state line. I was beginning to like the state more and more, as she revealed her unique beauty with each passing mile.

Escalante became the next scene in our Utah movie, as the forest thinned, and we descended out of the trees onto a massive mesa that stretched as far as the eye could see. We found ourselves riding on top of waves of pinkish-white rock. The highway appeared to be carved right into the sandstone, winding its way around like a boat slicing through a river current. The wide open 360-degree views looked surreal, almost man-made in the rock's cement-like appearance. The rolling rocks appeared to be water frozen in mid-flow—a huge beach compacted and solid.

The sun shone brightly, as we pulled over to try and capture the panorama around us. My legs ached, and I winced as I pushed myself up from the car seat and limped over to Alan and put my arms around his waist, as part affection and part crutch. The warm sun felt incredible on my face, and the gentle breeze blew through my hair. It was a perfect spring day. I stared hard at the rock valley in front of us, trying to focus on every detail and figure out how one could hike in this wild place. It was a maze; one I thought I'd never be able to escape once I found my way in. I wondered if I would ever return to experience such an adventure. The uncertainty of that answer made me shiver. I squeezed Alan's waist hard and rested my head on his chest, feeling the rise and fall of his stomach as he breathed. I wished we could just stay here, stop time, and just be.

The sun was sinking in the western sky, shrouded by clouds as we traveled our way along the winding road towards Zion National Park. It had been a full day on the road, with all our side trips and extra photo stops. Intermittent raindrops fell on the windshield, and we could smell the damp earth as the rain fell harder, sliding off the slick rock and making the rough stone shine in the dim light. The rock mounds on either side hemmed us in as the canyon narrowed. I gazed upward toward the sky and watched mini waterfalls cascading down the rock towers, streaming out from rock depressions. The streak of a permanent water stain marking their path. All along the rock's smooth edges sprang fountains of rainwater, as if someone designed this perfect water feature and turned on the faucet. The park is considered a semiarid desert climate, so it's ironic that we were there in the rain. But how special it was to see it rain in the desert and how quickly it pooled in the ditches and ran down the rocks. I could understand how flash floods could suddenly form.

We exited a short tunnel. The car hugged a wall of stone that curved around the switchback of the road, reminding me of the rounded walls of the Roman Coliseum. The wall was a massive block, with multiple waterfalls shooting from its top ledge. I couldn't say much as I gazed in awe at the enormous rock towers that shot straight up from the ground in shades of pink, orange, coal black, and sulfur red. It was like driving among grandiose fountains and majestic Roman architecture.

The following day we boarded a shuttle bus to the trailhead early in hopes of beating the crowds and the weather. Dense puffy clouds filled the sky, matching the rain forecast. I sat with my backpack on my lap, taking in the sights around me. I had never experienced a place like this before. The sheer canyon walls; their pink shades inching their way up the vertical rock faces with green bushes poking out. The top rim was nearly white, lopped off like a crew cut with green spikes of hair protruding from the top.

The bus's loudspeaker recording announced each rock formation and its name. Court of the Patriarchs; the Temples; Towers of the Virgin; the Altar of Sacrifice; and, finally, Angel's Landing, the destination of our hike. The canyon narrowed and it felt like we were riding through a cathedral closed in by stone walls adorned with colorful stained glass—a nave leading to the altar. The clouds and last night's rain created a somber mood that only ratcheted up the gloom filling my gut with dread. The rock formation's biblical names were omens of what was to come. I imagined my life being offered at the Altar of Sacrifice. My sins judged by the Court of Patriarchs. My prayers said before the Temples and Towers of the Virgin. And finally, my soul carried to Angel's Landing. I closed my eyes and inhaled deeply, whispering a prayer, feeling compelled to offer up my fears before the natural altars. I recalled college evenings in the stone chapel on campus, and the peace I found in its solid limestone structure. I had entered Mother Nature's chapel. I sensed I was here to lay my soul to rest.

The bus pulled into our stop for the trailhead. I stood up and immediately felt a twinge of pain in my knee, enough to jar me out of my morbid thoughts and back to the present moment. I assured myself that my legs could handle a five-mile hike.

We followed the trail across the river and began walking along thc base of the towering cliffs. The dirt path remained flat and gradually began to climb upward through a tight ravine. It was clearly a well-traveled route, although we were the only two from the bus who were walking its wide path. The dirt turned into patches of asphalt, as if someone had poured concrete rock mix on top of the ground. In my early morning fog, I initially assumed it was a natural rock path; I'd never seen a sidewalk in the wilderness, but indeed the surface had been paved by humans. My knee certainly did not appreciate the unforgiving asphalt as we began switchbacking up the side of the cliff; the metal tips of my hiking poles clinking with each step.

I watched the clouds as we slowly hiked our way up the trail. My legs felt like the cement we were walking on—heavy blocks of clunky and creaky joints and bones. I stopped frequently, feigning admiration or pointing out a formation just so I could catch my breath and give my legs a break. The clouds bubbled higher into the sky and marched slowly toward us. After last night's fountain show, I knew Mother Nature could turn those dry slides into gushing water cascades in a quick downpour; the kind of rain these billowing clouds could produce. I made a mental note of where my raincoat was stored in my pack, glad to have my clearance rack lavender jacket even if it made me look like an Easter egg when wearing it.

We reached the trail junction and followed as it snaked up the opposite wall, switchbacking, and gradually rising to the top of a flat ledge. To my surprise, a vault toilet located in an outhouse sat in the middle of the ledge. How fortuitous, but also, how crazy? A toilet perched atop this rocky cliff with sheer drop-offs on either side.

I needed to rest my tired legs and aching knee, so I took advantage of the toilet seat. Alan stood examining the route as I came up behind him.

"Do you think we'll make it?" I asked.

"I'm not sure. I don't like the look of those clouds."

I scanned the sky and scoped out the route that would take us up a narrow ridge of rocky sandstone to some point up above. The clouds grew darker as they gathered speed and rushed toward us like a tsunami.

"Let's wait here and see if the weather clears," he suggested.

"OK."

I half-wanted the sky to explode into driving rain so we could just go back down, but mostly I wished the clouds would merely drop their baggage and move onward. To clear up like they do back home so we could still get to the top and enjoy what's supposed to be a spectacular view.

We put on our rain jackets and waited for the rain. Little sprinkles splashed on our hats and within minutes a steady drizzle dampened the stone, steam rising from the rocks with that familiar wet rock smell. I hated that smell. We watched as the cliff walls darkened in their moistened state like they did the night before. Soon the waterfalls began appearing. First, a dribble from one cleft in the rock and then more appeared, and finally a steady flow streamed down the rocks like tears. I watched in awe as the dusty dry sandstone soaked up the rain, turning a deep rust color. The desert landscape quickly became wet and humid. It was an amazing sight; that area gets less than 1 inch of rain on average in the month of May, and this was our second rain event in 24 hours. We stood still on the lookout platform and watched the storm clouds roll through the canyon, making their magic.

The canyon colors intensified, as the rain drizzled, making the green of the juniper and piñon pines more vibrant. The splashes of Indian Paintbrush evolved into bright flames sticking out of the cracks along the canyon wall. We watched as the clouds began to dissipate off to the south, and blue sky began to peak through in the distance. Maybe we would still get a chance to reach the top.

Alan wrapped an arm around me. "Isn't this gorgeous? Look at those waterfalls. How many people get to see this?"

I'd guess not many, other than the handful of people waiting on the outhouse rock. Normally we wouldn't see this either, as fair-weather, lightning-averse hikers. Forecasts like today would have generally kept us off the trails. Previously, I had experienced the tingling sensation of electricity and my hair standing on end as lightning struck close by while hiking up to Pikes Peak—it wasn't something I wanted to repeat. Yet here we were on vacation with limited time and a set schedule; we just had to be prepared for the crazy weather.

We stood around for a few minutes to let the storm finish its dazzling show and for the waterfalls to recede away. The remaining clouds looked like the quintessential fluffy cotton balls you see in paintings. A few people started making their way up the trail. I looked at Alan, and he shrugged his shoulders.

I kept my rain jacket on as we followed the others up the trail. Still unsure how we were going to climb up this steep tower, I continued to put one foot in front of the other and paid close attention to where those feet were landing as we hugged the cliffside. With only a few bushes and some boulders clinging to the sides, I wasn't sure they would break our fall should one of us slip.

We met more people on their way down as we carefully maneuvered past one another. At probably the worst possible place to meet other hikers, we came upon a group of five young people. Mostly clad in shorts, t-shirts, and regular running shoes, they were figuring out how to navigate a huge step down along a slick rounded rock toward a larger rock shelf below. We waited on the shelf, watching as they nervously tried to slide down on their backsides only realizing that without something to hold onto, their slide could potentially send them hurtling like those spouts of water shooting off the rock into the abyss. I made a mental note about this treacherous section and studied the area for any type of hold or better way to descend than they were doing.

They finally glimpsed a little ledge that shortened the big step downward, and the group finally passed us and went on their way. I easily scrambled up the section and waited for Alan. Our route continued in this scrambling fashion as we moved higher toward the ridge that we'd seen from the platform below. Solid steel chains were bolted into the rock, creating a handrail for what otherwise is pure slick rock. Amazed at the effort the park had made to provide these climbing aids, I thanked whoever was crazy enough to come up with this idea, and grabbed on to the chain railing.

"How would we ever get up here without these?" I pondered aloud, glancing back at Alan as he held onto the metal railing.

"I know. Look at the drop-offs. Even with the chains, this is wild!"

We climbed the last pitch and found ourselves on the narrow cliff ledge known as Angel's Landing. I gazed down upon the glorious green valley below, with the winding river sliding around the cliffs. I walked out to the far edge and peered over the side, a little flutter occurred in my stomach as I leaned over the sheer cliff and saw a bus making its way up the canyon. It looked like a tiny toy car. I stepped backward and looked around for a place to sit, finding a perfect rock to sit on as I looked out toward the valley. I swung my pack around and placed it on the ground, then sat down to rest. Gazing out at the valley stretching out before us, I felt peace wash over me on my high perch. I closed my eyes, picturing the angels lifting my fears and carrying them away on their wings. The warm sun seeped into my cold dark voids of fear.

I imagined that my next trip would be in a little box, tucked deep in Alan's pocket, as he scrambled his way to the top. Once there, he could take a handful of my ashes and toss them into the breeze for the angels to carry into the sky. I stared out at the scene before me, trying to memorize every rock, every tree, every patch of blue sky and puff of white clouds. I knew I would not be back here, not in my physical form.

---

The next day we hiked a gorgeous trail to another lookout with even bigger canyon views. The trail again resembled a sidewalk, and my knee ached from pounding my feet on the hard surface. We hiked over to the river and sat on a rock at the river's edge. I slipped off my boots and socks, rolled up my pants as far on my thigh as they would go, and waded a few feet into the water and knelt down. The icy water soothed my aching joints and temporarily numbed their pain.

I looked downward and watched the river water flow through my hands. Little ripples were created by my fingers as it flowed around them. I closed my eyes and prayed silently for strength to endure whatever pain might be coming—whatever the lumps on my body might signify.

"Oh my gosh, does this feel good," I groaned, looking over at Alan who chose to stay on the rock and only dip his feet in the water. He smiled back, camera in hand, and snapped a picture. I tried to smile, tried to act like this was just another post-hike ice bath, while I wondered if this was the last natural soaking and perhaps one of the last pictures he'd ever take of me. I peered up toward the sky, hoping to find the answer written somewhere above.

Finally succumbed to the cold, I pulled myself out of the water to sit on a smooth rock bench and dry off. The sky was gloriously blue, and the leaves on the cotton-wood trees gently swayed in the breeze. I did not want this moment to end. We sat in silence as I continued to memorize the landscape before me; the smooth flow of the river, the cottonwood trees guarding the precious water that flowed beneath its branches. I scanned the canyon walls, noting how many trees and plants jutted out from tiny cracks in the sandstone, marveling at their tenacity to cling to life in their precarious perches, a near-vertical slab of lifeless rock. I heard laughter and water splashing as children and parents nearby waded in the cool water. Life abounded within these high canyon walls. I breathed in deeply, trying to capture and draw in the energy that surrounded me. I kept silently praying.

After our river dip, we boarded the shuttle bus as it rounded the bend and rode it to the last stop: the beginning of the popular Narrows trail. We had planned to only walk to the point where the trail is submerged by water as the canyon walls close in more tightly until there's no space for a path. It wasn't a long walk—just 2 miles or so round trip. I sat on the bus trying to muster the energy to force my feet to walk yet another 2 miles. As we disembarked, a sharp pain shot down the outer part of my knee. I was exhausted and now limping. I really wanted to see the Narrows, knowing it could be my final opportunity, but my knee throbbed. I kept longingly gazing over at the river and the rocks lining the edge, wanting to sit and watch the water.

After a few limping steps I confessed to Alan that I just couldn't make myself walk another 2 miles. I couldn't believe I said no to a hike, especially to a place as unique and iconic as the Narrows. I tried blaming my marathon fatigue, but I knew it really was something more.

I encouraged him to go on by himself, to which he reluctantly agreed. I watched as he walked down the trail alone, with tears brimming in my eyes. I headed towards the river and found a place to sit by the water, resting my chin in my hands. A curved rock wall following the bend in the river stood before me, its black stains streaking downward from its top to bottom. Ravens flew overhead. I searched for green trees or any plant life sticking out from the stone, but only viewed the dark streaks on the wall and flashes of the black birds.

I learned during my first Utah backpacking trip that the raven is important to Native American spirituality. I thought the raven was supposed to be a good sign, but I couldn't remember the story the guide told us. A slight breeze blew through the shadowed canyon. It felt like death's cold whisper—the raven and grim reaper. I brooded with my fate and let the darkness settle into my entire body. My shoulders dropping and head resting in my hands until fear and uncertainty filled every fiber of my being. The canyon's stark beauty was a direct contrast to the foreboding in my heart. I held death and life in my gaze and prayed before the black-stained altar of sandstone. I didn't know what lay ahead, but I prayed for the strength to fly as gracefully as the ravens. A gentle breeze again blew, and the ravens dipped, twisted, and floated above the canyon walls and out of sight. My prayers and fear followed their path skyward.

---

The next day we had breakfast at the diner and headed towards Bryce Canyon. While driving to the park, I received the dreaded call from the doctor confirming that I had metastatic melanoma. I really *was* going to be leaving this earth, just as my cousin Carla had done.

As I stood at the overlook gazing at the sea of orange rock lighting up the canyon, I felt at peace with my life. Carla's death had prompted me to say the sorrowful words I needed to say to my siblings. Even if this cancer killed me, I no longer worried about what my funeral would look like. I knew I wasn't bringing my tortured feelings along with me. I could fly freely like the ravens.

However, I dreaded telling my parents that I was sick. Another daughter with cancer—again. I'd always been the self-sufficient one, not wanting or needing anything, even from them. How could I tell them I might be dying?

"I should call them, shouldn't I?" I asked Alan that evening as I tried to eat a chicken sandwich that tasted like rubber. We were sitting in the hotel room attempting to be normal, hours after our lives had turned upside down because of one phone call.

"You probably should," he quietly responded.

"I don't know what to say." I didn't think I could even tell them the truth.

I mulled over the possibilities and decided to keep my conversation vague. I told my mom that the lump removed before the race was melanoma. She asked about the next steps, and I only mentioned that I'd need more tests. She seemed worried and nervous but thankfully wasn't overly emotional.

My nonchalant reference to melanoma was similar to when I'd told my parents about the mole I had removed when I was 27 years old. But that was just a mole, and it hadn't spread. This time, I'd left out a key detail—it was *metastatic* melanoma.

On the final day of our vacation, I heard Alan get up and figured I'd better get out of bed so we could get to the trailhead in time to take one last hike before heading back to Colorado. I was so exhausted, and my body felt like it had been hit by a truck. I really just wanted to sleep, but I also wanted to get out on the hike that many reviews said was the "best in the park".

"Can I open the shades?" he inquired.

"Sure."

He slid the thick curtains to the side, allowing bright sunshine to stream through the room. Finally, a sunny day! I was really getting tired of the ominous clouds and gray skies.

"I'm going to go gas up the car so we can just hit the road after our hike."

"Sounds good. I'll get my stuff packed."

I slipped on the same pair of hiking pants I'd been wearing for the past few days and pulled the bright-blue long-sleeved shirt out of my bag, the last clean shirt for the week. I brushed my teeth and gathered up my razor, soap, and hairbrush from the bathroom. I grabbed my boots from the corner and sat on the edge of the bed. My feet simply did *not* want to be back in my boots, nor did my legs want to hike. My knee still throbbed, and I was beginning to worry that I was doing permanent damage to it by hiking. I then paused, realizing that my body could be dead and gone in a mere few months. I could completely blow my knee out and it wouldn't matter. *Shit.* I was scheduled to have a PET scan in 2 days and an MRI following that to determine just how far the cancer has spread. I didn't know how many more hikes I would really be able to do.

Shoving my feet into my boots, I tightly cinched them and stood up. The now-familiar wave of fear rose upward from my toes and threatened to spill out in a rush of tears. I shoved my pajamas into my overnight bag, jammed my red toiletry case into its corner, and pushed everything down to zip it shut.

Alan hadn't returned, and I couldn't figure out why it was taking him so long to get gas. I paced the room, cursing my body and the entire situation. I was afraid to go home but knew I couldn't stay and avoid reality. I was terrified of sitting still. Paralyzed by a loneliness that I'd never felt before, and a neediness that repulsed my independent self.

I looked out the window to see Alan pulling into a parking space at the bottom of the hotel's outdoor stairs. He wore a gray shirt and khaki pants, and his blonde hair glistened in the sun. The same outfit he'd worn on so many other hikes. All our perfect days summiting peaks and sharing hundreds of trail miles together. I'd finally met a man who enjoyed the same simple and pure joy of being outside. We previously hiked under full moons and at first light. Navigated mountains with no trails, with only vague descriptions of which gully to ascend to reach the proper ridge and scramble to the top.

Alan was the first man I didn't try to impress or alter my ways to match his. I didn't worry about what he thought. I committed to being myself and accepting it if he didn't like me. I confessed to him the raw truth of my past, in addition to the counseling I had received to deal with it. I slowly laid all my cards on the table, wondering which would cause him to fold and call it quits. Yet, he was still here. And I loved him more than I thought I could ever love a human being. I desperately wanted him to stay, but couldn't ask him to endure the suffering

I knew was coming. How could I have found and fallen in love with someone *only* to have our first vacation be our last? I had convinced him to take this weeklong trip, knowing that we both needed a break, hoping we'd rediscover those carefree days of our first dates. And now I was dying. Like in some tragic Shakespearean play. I didn't want to put him through this.

He poked his head in the door. "Are you ready?"

"Yep. Let's get going."

---

We stood at the top of the rim and observed the endless blue sky with its cotton-ball clouds. The canyon orange rocks were glowing in the sunshine.

"It's even more beautiful today, if that is possible," he exclaimed.

"I know. I'm glad we finally got a 'bluebird' day."

The sandy trail squashed under our boots with yesterday's moisture, as we followed it out onto the shoulder where it switched back down, deeper into the canyon. I kept one eye on the trail, and the other on all the imaginary animals and buildings I could "see" in the rock's natural architecture. The same energy I felt the day before returned, along with the same clarity of vision that made every detail stand out—every unique shape, texture, and color of the rocks. This canyon and its playfulness drew me inward, reminding me to play and enjoy—to even make believe. As a child I found shapes and animals in the clouds. That imagination returned once again, as a zoo of creatures appeared to be molded into the rocks: chickens and frogs, a beagle's nose, and floppy ears. We walked amid the rock castles and peered upward at the canyon wall's chess pieces and an army of soldiers lined up in perfect symmetry.

The landscape's colors and textures were surreal in their sandy orange color and fascinating erosion shapes. The rocks were porous and crumbly, looking as if I could rub them into dust with my fingers. They certainly didn't look like they had been standing for millions of years, appearing as if they could wash away in the next rainstorm.

The trail snaked its way downward into the canyon, and we hiked in the shade of the rock towers. We passed by two natural bridges, mysteriously suspended across the sandstone, somehow hanging on despite the canyon's eroded walls around them. *Amazing Mother Nature!* The trail leveled and opened into a juniper and pine forest sprinkled along the creek bed.

Alan stayed further behind than normal and appeared anxious during our hike. I slowed and marveled at the trees, and wondered how they could exist in this sandy soil and rocky towers. Desert plant life is more abundant than I once realized. From the flowers clinging to the walls of Zion, to these giant trees poking up between skyscraper rock formations, I began viewing the desert not as a dry and drab void, but as an area harboring life forms that I hadn't seen anywhere else. I marveled at their ability to survive and thrive in a tiny rock crevice, somehow finding enough moisture in the sandy soil to survive. Not to mention the unique insects and lightning-fast lizards who skittered across the rocks.

"I need to find a tree."

Ah! Now I knew why Alan seemed preoccupied. There might be more life in the desert than I thought, but there still aren't many private places to take care of any bodily needs, especially on a popular national park trail. Luckily, many people weren't about, as it was still early in the morning. I stopped to admire the juxtaposition of forest green and sunset orange as he wandered off trail for some privacy.

The path followed the creek bed until we turned onto the Peekaboo trail up through the next section of hoodoos and archways. The sun was high enough so we could walk in its warmth up the rust-colored path. My legs didn't want to go uphill, but one of the joys of canyon hiking is that the only way out is up. I focused my attention on the rocks and their random but perfect shapes. Their little windows and rounded spires. We gazed outwardly at the aptly named Wall of Windows, which reminded me of the magnificent cathedrals of Europe with their stained glass, although these windows were painted a solid sky blue.

I could view the rim above and knew we were getting close to Bryce Point, which was where we would follow the rim's trail back to the car. This was our last hike. As much as I wanted to stop the horrendous pain throbbing in my knee and sit and relax, I didn't want to leave the safe cocoon of the hoodoos or miss any picturesque details of this beautiful park that I knew I'd never see again. I kept reminding myself: *Take mental pictures. Look everywhere. See everything.*

The fairy castle we'd seen from the rim on the first day was now just a few feet from us. Its obvious castle shape now appeared as separate pinnacles of cream-colored orange rising to the sky. Our view widened with each step we took higher on the trail. We walked below the Wall of Windows towards the archway, which was an opening carved out of the rock as if someone intentionally created it for humans to pass through.

Alan stopped often to take pictures, which enabled me to rest often then walk ahead. He still seemed a little distracted, but I was in my own world trying to savor every moment and keep my mind from seeking out scary places. The views in front of me distracted me from my pain with all their Disney-like fantastical formations and animated pillars of stone. If my body wasn't screaming for rest, I would've likely kept walking forever.

After passing under the archway, the trail took a sharp switchback just below Bryce Point. I decided to stop and wait for Alan before continuing the climb upward to the rim. When I turned around, I was greeted by hundreds of bright candy-corn-colored statues, which were pocked by pine trees and covered with a blanket of blue sky and fluffy clouds. It was indeed the prettiest view in the entire park. An overwhelming sense of awe washed over me. Such beauty, and near humor, was celebrated in this figurative bowl of Halloween candy laid out before me. Something about its colors and shapes just made me smile.

Alan walked over and placed his arm around me. I leaned into him and squeezed his side. He began mumbling something about the park being amazing, and that he'd been trying to find the right time because he had a question he'd been meaning to ask. Standing there, not fully comprehending the rambling babble coming from his mouth, I wished that he'd be quiet so I could simply be in the moment. But those few words, "the right time," and "a question," made my mind race. Could he really be asking . . . . *Is he saying what I think he's saying*? As I started comprehending his words, I turned around to look at him, and he was bent down on one knee.

"Will you be my hiking partner for life?"

He'd barely finished his question when I threw my arms around him, nearly pushing him over like a linebacker tackling a quarterback. I was overjoyed, and surprised, and overwhelmed, all at once. We hugged and cried, and just held each other on that little strip of dirt. The rest of the world disappeared as I buried my head in his shoulder and held on tightly.

Finally, I let go and stood back up. He reached into his pocket, took out a simple silver ring with a single purple stone, and held it up to me.

"Where did you get this?"

"That's why it took me so long to get gas."

The gift shop in the resort hotel. It all made sense.

He slipped the ring on my finger, and I held out my arm to see what it looked like to have a ring on my left hand. It was perfect.

Saying yes was so easy. Especially when in the back of my mind I believed the commitment would be short, with our time together abbreviated by one of life's tragic endings. I could hardly believe that he really asked after my last day and a half of dark grieving. Part of me wanted him to marry me to solidify our relationship and commitment to each other. Yet, another part felt it unfair to make him go through this with me. I was so torn but so happy. I guess I didn't have to tell him that it was all right to leave me; thankfully he'd made that choice on his own.

---

A week after we returned from vacation, Alan and I sat in an exam room holding hands in silence. We were waiting for the doctor to confirm my fears that had been plaguing me the last few weeks. My mind swirled, wondering how the next few months would unfold. *Could we have a quick wedding? Would I die a fiancée and not a wife? How awful will the treatments be? Are my good days already gone, and will only suffering remain? Will I make it to 40?*

Soon the door opened, and a vivacious blonde walked in with my chart in her hand. My oncologist. I introduced her to Alan, then she sat down on the chair and wheeled over, positioning herself between the two of us—a triangle of bodies, our legs nearly touching. She oozed with compassion and her soft voice comforted my fearful soul.

She started with the good news—the brain MRI was clear. *Phew—one big bullet dodged.* I was relieved.

Then the bad news. I had lesions on my spine, liver, spleen, and adrenal glands. Not to mention all the subcutaneous lumps on my back, ribs, and everywhere else on my body.

In addition, spots on the tissue were present between my eyes. It's why my peripheral vision had started to disappear. I'd noticed it when we were hiking; my vision stopped abruptly as my eyes tried to focus to the far right or left of my view. It was as if I had something on the bridge of my nose, blocking my view. I could only see black, similar to when an optometrist covers your eyes with the spoon-like tool during an examination. I tried then to ignore my vision loss, and instead kept moving my eyes back and forth, hoping the dark spot was caused by my sunglasses or something otherwise obstructing my vision. I then thought I was imagining it. Now, I knew it was real! And it was the cancer. *Could it make me go blind?*

When the doctor examined me and asked about any vision problems, I lied. I'd said that I could see fine. I couldn't admit to my black spots.

Now I sat in disbelief as she pointed out the exact number of places where the cancer had spread. *How could I be alive and feel this good? All those places are vital organs. Cancer in the bone is never good.* I thought I could live without a spleen, but not my liver. And the PET scan didn't indicate whether the lump under my armpit was a metastatic lesion or if it was breast cancer.

I was in a very bad way.

I couldn't even look at Alan. This news was worse than I had ever imagined. I focused my eyes on the pages of typed descriptions of all those tumors she'd given me and just squeezed his hand. I was going to die. I felt hot and slightly nauseous. My heart beat fast as it seemed to be sinking down into my gut, dropping onto the floor, and falling through the 12 flights of stairs and into the building's basement. The weight of the dreadful news pressed me into the chair. I could not move my legs.

I finally lifted my head to ask the one question I needed to ask, although I already knew the answer. "This is stage four?"

The doctor tenderly looked at me with her gorgeous blue eyes and said, "Yes, it is stage four."

"But there is some good news," the doctor continued. "There are so many new developments in the treatment of melanoma." Then she flipped the pages of my stack of PET scan lesions to the list of all the treatment options.

I could hardly believe her. The first time I had melanoma treatments simply did not exist. A stage four diagnosis meant quick death. I hadn't kept up on any research though, so I was clueless about recent medical discoveries. I felt a twinge of hope and a flutter in my stomach.

She explained that chemotherapy and radiation simply were not effective. I had watched Jolene go through them both when she was 15 with leukemia, and it didn't look like much fun. The doctor wanted to test my blood to determine if I had a certain gene mutation which meant I was eligible for one of the treatment options. The gene mutation was BRAF. My frantic and desperate mind latched onto the mutation's name. My initials are RAF. *Surely, this was a good sign.* I needed something, anything, so I could hold onto my desperate need for hope.

She moved on to the next treatment on the list, Interleukin, or IL-2 for short. She explained that it was intense, but that I was a perfect candidate. IL-2 was a new immunotherapy designed to supercharge one's own immune system allowing it to attack the tumors. She described the treatment and research, enthusiastically pointing out that IL-2 was the only treatment shown to nearly cure the disease. Meaning that people lived beyond 5 years from their diagnosis. As she stated it, she took her pencil and wrote "5–7% cure" on my paper in perfect penmanship. *Cure.* I had no idea that word could even be used in the same conversation as metastatic melanoma. The tiny 5 to 7 percent did *not* register.

My legs moved as I was figuratively released from the chair's grip. My heart instantly leapt the 12 floors up and back into my body. *I could live. I will live. Oh my gosh, there is a potential cure.* My mind raced, and a smile spread across my face. This time I looked at Alan and squeezed his hand in hope instead of despair.

*Cure.*

The doctor referred me to the University of Colorado Hospitals (UCH), and she wanted me to see the leading researcher at their Melanoma Clinic. My treatment would be done at UCH. It required patients to have stress tests and lung functioning tests performed before they began treatment. She wrote up the order, but because I had recently run a marathon, she hoped they would waive those tests. I could discuss this with the melanoma doctor.

I walked out of the doctor's office floating on clouds surrounded by blue sky. I felt so different from prior days, when I was followed by thunder and lightning bolts, ready to strike me at any second. I knew I was going to *live.*

Alan and I decided to get a cup of coffee and visit a nearby park. It was a beautiful spring day, and I couldn't quite go back to work. I needed to feel the fresh air and warm sun on my face. I needed to thank the universe, the mountains, and Mother Nature for giving me hope.

I also knew I needed to call my parents. They knew I was visiting the doctor and would let them know the results. I punched their number in my phone and waited for my mother's sing-song hello on the other end. Again, I glossed over all the tumor details, just indicating there are spots in multiple places as if they were inconsequential.

"But there is a new treatment, and I am a great candidate," I quickly told her. I had to keep the conversation as light and breezy as possible. I couldn't bring myself to tell the real truth. It would devastate her, and then I would have to bear her anxiety in addition to my own. I was already having a hard time keeping myself afloat. I couldn't add anyone else on my shaky raft. It was best to stay positive—and vague.

———

Another week later, Alan and I sat again in the exam room holding hands at the university hospital. There was a big poster illustrating the stages of melanoma on the back of the door. I looked down at the bottom of the list at stage four, where it simply stated that the tumors have spread to distant organs. That's me. The bottom rung. I couldn't even remember what stage they said I was when I was 27. I believe it might have been IA or II.

I was anxious to hear more about the IL-2 treatment. I understood this doctor was one of the best in the country, and had led many of the new research trials. It had been 20 days since I got the call, and I was ready to do something about all my lumps and growing weakness.

The week before, I sat in my office trying to concentrate on the words on my computer screen when a colleague knocked on the door. I glanced to my right and

THE RUN OF MY LIFE

saw the big black blob between my eyes, and nodded to her as I tapped away at the keyboard trying to finish my thought. When I turned my chair towards her, she rattled off some questions about the upcoming meeting we were planning. My head felt fuzzy, and I could barely follow her conversation as she waited for an answer. My tongue turned into cement, and I strained to form the words flashing in my brain. A hot wave of fear washed over me, as I realized the source of my stammer. I tried focusing on her face and using as few words as possible.

In the back of my mind, I wanted to blurt out, *I have cancer. I'm dying. This meeting is pointless.* My body was being taken over, and I could do nothing but stammer and stutter and curse.

The doctor entered the room and shook our hands. He was bald with a salt-and-pepper mustache and dark eyes. His lips gave no hint of smile, just straight and serious. His nurse stood behind him and smiled widely as she introduced herself.

He sat down on the swivel chair at the desk next to me and swiped his badge to unlock the computer.

"It is a good time to have stage four melanoma," he said as he tapped the keys and scrolled through the screen.

*A good time to have stage four melanoma. Oh yes, I feel lucky. What is wrong with this man?* I thought, wanting to laugh at the absurdity of that statement but only cringing at the reminder of my diagnosis.

"There are many new treatment options," he said.

*That's what I've heard. And you're the one who knows the magic cure.* He clicked through a list of files, hovering his mouse over a document labeled "Patient Education" and opened a PowerPoint presentation. The first slide showed a figure wearing a dark hooded robe with a beak-like nose and black hat. The Grim Reaper, I assumed. I thought *this was a good time to have stage four melanoma?* I was struggling to like this doctor—the man who was supposed to save me.

The next slide was a simple graph. A line started at the top left of the screen, then took a deep dive nearly straight down to the bottom and arced sharply, before flattening out and stretching to the lower-right corner of the screen into an L shape. It was worse than any mountain incline I've ever hiked. I leaned in to read what the tiny numbers said on the chart. The line represented the number of people with metastatic melanoma, and the bottom axis was the amount of survival time following diagnosis. I looked closer and read that the time span was in months. The nosedive happened fast. Translation: The average life span was 9 months post-diagnosis. I felt the heat rise once again through my chest. My heart began pounding and then dropped, faster than the line nosedived on the screen.

He pointed to the flat part of the curve, the tail, as he called it. Those who can survive the precipitous slide tend to stay alive—but the tail only measured out to 36 months. My hope from the other doctor and her talk of cures completely flatlined. Tears began welling in my eyes. Blinking hard, I focused on the numbers on the screen and the treatment options he was explaining. I didn't want to let the Grim Reaper see me cry.

The doctor closed out the file, clicked on a screen with my name, and opened my PET scan images. I saw the outline of my skeleton as he scrolled quickly through my feet and legs. He teased me that my legs looked too small for a marathoner. I believe they must have put marathoner in capital letters on my medical chart, as everyone seemed to know. *At least he has some sense of humor.* He moved up through to my torso area and slowed the cursor. The black and white outline of my skeleton was dotted with pinkish blobs.

"These are tumors," he explained, pointing to all the spots. "This is your liver, spleen. These are on your spine."

My breathing slowed with every new spot.

He scrolled up to my head and put the cursor on the little blobs between my eyes. I looked at my nose and saw the black shadow—the blobs in real life.

The last image showed my whole body. It looked like the outline of a dark Christmas tree with pink lights. I asked about the lumps on my arm and neck, and where they are on the screen. He scrolled back through the images but couldn't see them.

"They are too small to show up on the PET," he matter-of-factly stated.

*Too small.* That means all these other tumors are big enough to see, feel, and touch. *Bigger than the lumps under my skin that I touch every day?* My eyes got wider as I grasped the reality of all those pink spots. It felt real and scary on paper, but seeing it on the screen—my body riddled with tumors--made me clutch Alan's hand even harder as I tried to take it all in.

The doctor turned and looked at me, and then at Alan.

"Let's do the BRAF test to see if you're eligible for that treatment, but you are the perfect candidate for IL-2," he said. He explained the process; I'd be in the hospital for 5 days in a sub-intensive care unit. He said it will feel like having a bad case of the flu, and that I would gain a lot of fluid weight. It could also cause my heart to race and blood pressure to drop, but I am young and in good shape. He says we can skip the heart stress test and lung functioning tests given my marathoner status.

"It probably won't work, but it is worth a try. This is your only shot at a home run."

It probably won't work.

A home run.

I focused on home run. *Cure. Five to seven percent. I can do this.* I looked over at Alan and turned back to the doctor.

"Let's do the IL-2. When can we start?"

He looked over at his nurse, and they agreed to start the following week. He discussed some of the research protocol and the clinical trials. He wasn't sure if I would be officially enrolled, and he may want lab work and other tests. I assumed this was all to put my data on the line in his PowerPoint presentation. I wanted to ride that curve until infinity.

The doctor stood up to leave and shook our hands. "I'll see you in the hospital next week."

The nurse stayed behind to go over all the paperwork and get everything scheduled. She was a petite brunette with beautiful green eyes.

"He can be pretty gloom and doom," she commented. I half-laughed at the obvious description and felt myself relax a little. She emanated compassion through her sweet eyes and gentle smile.

"Stay positive," she encouraged. "We've seen great results with this treatment."

She was the angel companion to the Grim Reaper.

She sat in the doctor's chair and walked through everything again. The flu-like symptoms. The heart and blood pressure concerns. The fluid retention. She told me to bring a baggy pair of pants to wear after discharge, as I could be up to 20 pounds heavier. This is not the time for skinny jeans, she said (as if I own a pair of skinny jeans). I was grateful for her humor.

She handed me a folder thick with pamphlets and brochures. "Metastatic Melanoma Conversation Kit: Have the Conversation of a Lifetime" neatly printed across the front. Inside were documents on treatment options and what to expect. Another folder contained general cancer information. How to deal with a terminal illness. Getting your financial papers in order. Legal documents. Talking to your family.

We spent the rest of the time discussing my end-of-life wishes and filling out the green form stating my requests for the hospital. It all seemed so surreal, talking about my end-of-life treatment desires as if I were choosing between ordering chicken or steak for dinner. I was calm and confident in my answers. I had thought about these decisions many times, especially in the last few months.

*Damn*, I thought to myself. *Why didn't I do all these things after Carla died like I said I would?* I was going to do them "just in case." Three months later, and just in case had actually arrived.

My mind raced between hope and despair as we walked out of the cancer center. I kept seeing home runs and long tails, and then steep drop-offs and black-beaked grim reapers. I wasn't sure which would be true, but my heart put its bet on home runs. Despite my upbringing as a Cubs fan and their perennial losing record, I believed in home runs even in the bottom of the ninth inning with a 3–2 count and two outs.

I held Alan's hand as we made our way to the car. Our silence and tightly squeezed fingers was becoming our ritual for absorbing medical facts and fantasy dreams of miracles.

## *five*

# Finding Handholds

fter receiving the details of my diagnosis and the odds of treatment being successful, I knew there was no question that I could die. Soon. Forty could be a pipe dream. And my birthday was a mere 4 months away. This was a big deal.

I always handled big deals by myself, especially bad deals. Bad news. Tragedy. I went off by myself. I cried alone in the school bathroom when my sister was sick. I was alone when I got the news that my grandmother had passed. I went back to work and a long run after I found out I had melanoma the first time, not telling anyone until hours later. I didn't ask Alan to come to my house after my cousin died. I had been conditioned to carry my pain alone. It was not worth sharing. Surely others had greater problems than I.

But this was different. I couldn't keep this to myself. I knew this was a challenge that I could not beat on my own. I could not do this alone. Besides, I didn't care if it ruined my image as a stubborn, independent woman. I was going to die so it didn't matter. Nothing mattered. Other than trying to live. The rest of my world was irrelevant. I suddenly didn't care what people thought of me.

I tapped out an email and addressed it to all my friends and family, giving them a condensed version of the last few years. Some of the people on my list hadn't heard from me in a long time. Throwing caution to the wind and risking lots of "who cares" or just plain silence, I hit send. Looking back on my note, it was pretty vague. No mention of stage four, the survival curve (or cliff would be a better description), and nothing about death or goodbye. Rather a simple, *Hey, I'm engaged, almost qualified for Boston.* I sprinkled in the bad news as if it were just a minor hiccup in the otherwise dreamy state of my life.

My inbox pinged with new messages. Some were short, with congratulations and good-luck messages. Others were longer and deeper responses with encouraging words and pep talks. *You've got this. Cancer has nothing on you.* Magical thinking for sure, but I also wanted to believe in that magic. Even if they didn't believe what they wrote, the words built upon my fierce desire to live.

Eventually, letters, cards, emails, books, games, bridal magazines, and even stuffed animals piled up on my kitchen table. People I barely knew, or didn't know at all but were friends of my family, or friends of friends, sent notes and encouraging words.

I was surprised by the names on the return address labels. I had moved a lot in my 20s and 30s. At nearly every family gathering when I was asked what I was doing, I answered with the title of a new job. I would have liked to say I was "finding myself," but in reality I was running away from myself; running away from a past I didn't want to bring along to my future. The little girl crying on that rainy April day. The angry teenager who wanted nothing to do with mothering, parenthood, or men. The young woman who dealt with unhealthy friendships and boys who took advantage of her.

I had worked hard to create a new identity, hoping to rip off the label of crybaby pushover and replace it with something else—something more capable and confident. Yet my old self followed me everywhere as I moved on and left people behind. I didn't keep in touch with childhood friends, high-school classmates, or even my college roommate, with whom I shared some of the best and darkest days of my life. The only way I could seem to keep myself afloat was to blot everyone out. To keep running away.

I built a wall around myself, believing it would separate me from the past and keep me safe. I wanted nothing more than a life without feelings, sterile and free of messy relationships. My work in the heady policy world was the perfect match. The suit I wore was not just a business uniform but a way to stay in my head and leave the heart behind. It was my protective shield; my way of coping and adapting.

Many of the people that I had turned away from were now sending me letters and text messages. Word spread beyond my initial list of recipients; friends I hadn't seen or talked to in years reached out. Their generous words and gestures were a keen reminder of the power of grace. Free and undeserving favor. Humbling and heartening examples of the human spirit and its need for connection. That little girl who wanted to cry so many years ago was the same woman crying now in gratitude for being held in that moment—fears and all.

My heart had started opening before Carla died, expanded after her death, and was breaking wide open as I faced my own mortality. I still owe a debt of gratitude to all the people who prayed for me, sent notes, or just shared hope for a miracle.

---

Warm metal-free clothes. No food or anything to drink, other than water, for 6 hours before the scan. Low-carb diet for 24 hours prior. No exercise either. It was another element of the nightmare I was starting to live. No exercise and no carbs! For an exercise addict, that is pure torture.

I scoured my closet and drawers for metal-free pants. I assumed any pair of sweats would work, hoping that my best pair would fit the bill. I picked them up and looked at the drawstring. *Damn.* It had a metal grommet around the hole for the drawstring. So did the next pair, and the next. I was getting worried I wouldn't have an appropriate pair of pants. I certainly didn't feel like shopping. And why would I buy anything new? I was dying. Who needed new pants that would only be worn for a few months?

Finally, the last pair I picked up did not have any metal grommets, zippers, buttons or anything metal anywhere. Phew—at least one crisis is averted.

Now for a top to wear. Something warm. Apparently, it's cold in the scan machine. I grabbed the purple fleece sweatshirt my honey bought me. It wasn't my favorite, but it certainly is warm, and I thought it would be a good omen.

I woke early for the seven o'clock appointment for my scan, and drove across town to the hospital that could fit me in on such late notice. I walked into the building, and it wasn't at all what I expected. The walls were painted a deep shade of blue. A handful of dark leather chairs were scattered about the waiting room. It was almost a homey feeling. It just needed a fireplace, and I could've curled up with a nice book and felt like I was in someone's cozy den. It wasn't like the sterile white-light hospital rooms or doctor offices I'd been in before.

The receptionist kindly took my information and handed me forms. I nervously filled them out, but when I got to the marital status question, I froze. I had been proudly marking Single all these years, but today I wanted to blurt out—I'm engaged. Where's the box for that?

*I'm not single. I'm not a lonely young woman going through a terminal illness by herself. Really, I have someone who cares about me. Who loves me. Who is going to be with me through this. I want them to know that. Why can't I mark that somewhere on this sheet? Dammit. I don't want them to think I'm single.*

I looked down at my temporary engagement ring, the simple silver band with a purple stone. No one would know this is an engagement ring. No one knows that

I am not alone. Especially because it's on my middle finger; Alan had guessed the size, and it was a little on the big side.

I returned the forms to the receptionist, and resisted the temptation to tell her that the form needed another box. They included divorced, widowed, and separated. Why not engaged?

I hadn't realized until that moment the power of that symbol. The ring. I always thought I'd just want a simple silver band. I really thought the purple middle-finger ring would suffice. Or that I didn't really need a ring at all. I am a simple person and not a flashy jewelry wearer. I wear the same necklace, earrings, and rings every day.

But that day I decided I wanted diamonds. I wanted a ring like my mother's—a center diamond with smaller ones on each side. I wanted a ring that clearly said I was taken. That said I was going to be someone's wife. And more importantly, that I had a companion on this journey.

For the first time in my life, I wanted nothing to do with being single. Cancer had not only turned my health upside down, but it also clearly flipped my self-identity.

A tech called my name and took me back to the scanning area. He directed me to a spacious room with another leather chair, soft lighting, plenty of magazines, and a television. I guess if you're dying, they figure you might as well be comfortable.

He asked a few friendly questions. The chart said I had just run a marathon. Which one, he inquired. Of course, he was also a runner. When he felt he had asked enough non-medical questions to calm my nerves, he asked the harder ones. When were you diagnosed? Did the doctor explain why you needed a PET scan? When is your MRI scheduled? And your doctor appointment?

Then he explained the process. First, the injection of a radioactive sugar substance that would attach to any cancer cells and show up as lighted areas on the PET scan. He said I shouldn't have any side effects; it would feel a little cold going in, but I shouldn't feel anything else. The injection needed time to circulate through the system, so I would sit for about an hour before they'd take me back for the scan. The doctors ordered a full body scan, so it would be two separate processes. He explained that they would do the top part of my body first, and then the lower half. The whole process would take about 2 hours. One hour waiting and about 45 minutes for the scans. He asked if I had any questions.

"Um, no, I guess not. Other than, can you tell me how many lit areas you see?"

He gave a slight but pained smile. "No, I cannot. The results will be sent to a radiologist to read the scans. Your doctor will get the results."

I assumed as much, but thought I'd ask. He was kind of cute. Maybe he'd want to give this "single" girl a heads up.

I tried to relax in the comfy leather chair, but my mind was a little chaotic. It had been easier to stay distracted when we'd been in Utah, focusing on the natural world. To put one foot in front of the other on the trails. This quiet room provided too much space for real thoughts. Real fear and worry. Thankfully, the cute tech turned on a documentary for me to watch. It was about glaciers or something. I just remember the beautiful scenery, the blue shades of ice, and crystal-clear pools. I was happy to have nature to gaze upon as I tried to ignore the fear.

I was not only worried about what would show up, but also concerned that I was going to freak out during the scan. The nurse asked if I was claustrophobic, to which I answered, "Yes, a little."

She explained that I would be lying down, and that the machine would wrap around you like you are lying in a tube. I could only remember those times my brother would throw a blanket over my head and I'd panic. Or any time I'd feel trapped in any way. I was trying to figure out a way to calm myself, or a mantra to say in my head, to pass those 45 minutes in the tube. I wasn't sure what to expect, or how I'd react. I worried I would freak out, or not be able to do it at all.

The tech positioned me on the table with my head on a pillow, and one under my knees as well. He told me to put my arms above my head and to, of course, stay very still. He covered me with a blanket and asked if I wanted to listen to music. I thought that might ease my mind, so I agreed. When he asked what type of music I wanted to listen to, I couldn't come up with anything. Sensing that I was overwhelmed with the simple question, he just asked what radio station I preferred. I conjured up enough brainpower to remember one of the programmed stations on my car radio.

As I waited for the scan to begin, I scoped out the true amount of room inside the capsule-like tube. I thought I would be fine. The top of the machine was at least 1 foot from my face if not more. The sides were 2 or 3 feet away.

I breathed a sigh of relief as the table moved, and my body went further into the tube. I closed my eyes before my head went in, imagining that I was near the glaciers I had just seen on the documentary. I kept telling myself, *I am going to be OK. Just breathe. Be still. Know that the universe is never wrong.*

I was grateful for all the Buddhist readings I had done, as well as my consistent practice of meditation over the prior years. I was able to remain calm and still in the tube. I focused on my breath and pictured myself on the top of a mountain pass with nothing but blue sky and high peaks before me. I breathed in my fear and breathed out hope. I imagined ice-blue glaciers and snow-capped mountains. These beautiful images kept me away from the dark thoughts of suffering and death.

Yet, my happy thoughts were being interrupted by the growing tingling sensation I felt in my arms. Having them over my head was becoming quite uncomfortable, and they were starting to go numb. I had no idea how long I had been inside the tube, but I hoped it was getting close to the 20-minute mark. I tried to concentrate on my mountain visions, breathing, and remaining calm. The urge to move my arms was getting hard to resist. The tingling took over my thoughts until it was hard to remain focused on my mountains. Thankfully, I felt the table start to exit the machine, and the room lights penetrating my eyelids. The door opened, and I heard the tech walking towards me.

"You can move. The first part is over."

I sighed with relief, as I brought my arms down and rested them on my stomach.

The second half of the scan was much easier. I could keep my arms at my side, and I didn't have to worry about sneezing or doing anything else with my upper body that would mess up the image. Before long, I was being escorted back to the comfy waiting area. The tech offered me some coffee, juice, and a granola bar.

"We assume everyone is hungry after fasting. I hope you're a coffee drinker."

"Yes, I am. Thanks." I was starving and definitely going through caffeine withdrawal.

He stuck out his hand and looked me in the eye, "Good luck to you." I sensed in the pace of his words and his lingering handshake that he saw lots of highlighted areas, and that he knew I was in for the fight of my life.

I thanked him, my eyes welling with emotion and gratitude, and walked out into the bright sunshine.

I drove to Alan's townhouse, dejectedly walked up to his door, and knocked. He quickly came and held it open, as I stepped up and slid my arms around his waist. He hugged me tightly and asked how it went. I gave him the rundown of the process, and told him the tech had even asked about my marathon.

I sat on his couch wanting to tell him about the paperwork's marital status question, and it not having a box to check for "engaged." But I couldn't bring myself to admit—or to boldly ask—for a big fat diamond! Especially after I'd told him I was completely satisfied with my purple gem.

"So, what do you want to do the rest of the day?" I had taken the day off, knowing I wouldn't be in the head space to work. And at that point, I didn't care if I ever walked into my office again.

"I don't know," I said, fiddling with my ring, trying not to look down.

"Do you want to go ring shopping?"

Had I been that obvious? Had I subliminally communicated my secret ring desires?

I looked up and shrugged my shoulders, trying to contain my excitement and pretend it wasn't that big of a deal. "I guess we could."

"Let's do it. What else are we going to do?"

He squeezed my hand and stood up, pulling me up with him.

I looked down at my nasty drab white t-shirt, my A-cup boobs drooping in their metal-free freedom. It was the only bra I owned without an underwire that wasn't a sausage-casing sports bra. I wore no makeup per the scan instructions, and had pulled back my hair in a ponytail. While I wasn't looking my best, I also knew that I was ready to do this ring thing. Outfit be damned! I was ready to mark something other than "single" on those medical forms. I was ready to have a ring, a visible symbol that I was not alone. I had a fiancé—despite my flat chest, cheap clothes, and terminal diagnosis.

---

I have always felt a little inadequate in my role as a woman. I've never been very girly, preferring jeans and sweatshirts to dresses and skirts. I didn't wear much makeup, despite embracing the 80's pastel pink and blue eyeshadow as a high schooler, along with perfectly permed hair and lots of hairspray. I drew the line at eyeliner and foundation—I couldn't quite master the application process. I relied on a little blush for my cheeks and maybe some mascara.

At the jewelry store, the salesperson asked what kind of cut I preferred. What type of metal and style? I looked at Alan, then back at the salesperson, feeling my head drop and the excitement drain from my face. I wanted to walk right back out the door. I stumbled and stammered, and finally just admitted I wasn't sure what she meant by cut or style. I tried to play off my ignorance, but my flushed face and stunned eyes surely gave away my total lack of preparation.

This wasn't something that I'd ever thought about. Heck, I never thought I'd be getting married. It hadn't been on my to-do list, and a diamond wasn't something I even secretly shopped for. According to the look on the saleswoman's face, I clearly was failing the newly engaged test, and felt I must have missed out on an important class. Was there a quiz I should have taken before saying yes? A handbook to read? A how-to-pick-out-a-diamond guide to peruse? I just wanted to tell her that I wanted a ring like my mother's. Her ring was simple yet classy, with one larger diamond and smaller ones on either side. I couldn't quite picture the metal—was it gold? Silver? I thought gold, but could also see silver in my brain. What style? I didn't know—1960's classy. Cut—I had no idea. I could only recall one larger diamond surrounded by a few smaller ones. Why wasn't I more prepared?

I wanted to blurt out, I'm dying. I just came from a PET scan, which is why my boobs are sagging and

116                                          THE RUN OF MY LIFE

I look like crap. I haven't really had a lot of time to ponder rings.

By the end of the excursion, I was exhausted. Who knew there are a million ways to design a ring?

---

The complete flipping of my life scripts continued as I entered the advice stage—when everyone had ideas about how to cure my cancer and deal with the emotions that went along with it. Normally, I'd have eaten up the suggestions, eager for approval. I would have jumped right in, happy to have someone else lead the way. Self-help books lined my bookshelves, and I've always sought other perspectives. I took pride in my ability to get permission rather than beg for forgiveness. People said I was a good girl. I did what I was told, and thrived on the praise associated with my steadfast obedience.

People tried to tell me what to eat and drink, how much to sleep, whether I should continue working, books I should read, medical research to study, which brand of lotion I should use, and what kind of socks I should wear in the hospital. My favorite was when someone told me I should take my diagnosis more seriously. Really? Evidently, I was laughing too much for a person with incurable stage four cancer. Go figure.

Even my doctors didn't give me that much advice. When I asked if there was anything I should be doing or not doing, my doctor and nurse both shook their heads. When I pressed them on whether I could have a glass of wine, the nurse looked at me with a sympathetic smile,

"I think you could have a bottle." (*Thank you. I think I'll do that.*)

I knew the suggestions arose from concern for me, and that everyone wanted to help me get better. And if they felt they knew what would help me heal, they wanted to let me know. I love them for that. They cared enough to tell me that they wanted me to live.

I wished it were that easy, though. But in my heart of hearts, I knew that well wishes would only get me so far. It's not that I didn't need or want help. The amount of information coming at me was simply overwhelming. The large folder stuffed with pamphlets and brochures about talking to your family, getting your legal and financial papers in order. The human resources paperwork for taking time off. Insurance forms. It was all overwhelming.

Other questions swirled in my head. *Should we plan a quick wedding? What was I going to tell my boss and my staff? Who was going to take care of my dog after I died? And what was I going to do with all the meetings on my calendar?*

Suddenly it hit me—if I was going to die, then what the hell! I could do whatever I wanted. None of this would matter in 6 or 9 months when I'm laid out in a wooden box or scattered into the wind.

So, I did whatever I wanted. I ate my normal diet, which was relatively healthy anyway. My bedtime remained the same. Work only stopped when I was too drugged to function or hospitalized. I continued to hike high peaks and bike to work. I still walked my dog around the neighborhood.

Reading medical information was out of the question. Who cares about PD-1 blockers or T-cells, or even how to pronounce the full drug names when you've been told they probably won't work? I did use the lotions and socks people gave me. And I also kept laughing, living, and loving life.

Don't get me wrong, I was scared shitless. The average survival was a mere 9 months. But no amount of food, sleep, or research statistics calmed my fears. Those fears were mine—all mine—and I had to find my own way to keep from falling apart, or worse, giving up completely. This was my cancer. My life at stake. As much as I would have liked a guide, I was on my own. Blazing a new trail on a mountain that I never wanted to climb. One step at a time.

The first steps taken were brutal. Week one of the treatments knocked me down. I spent 4 nights in the hospital, getting infusions every 8 hours. The resulting shaking and chills required high doses of painkillers to control. I was mostly out of it. Alan stayed with me, sleeping on the pleather couch opposite my bed. I felt bad for him but so grateful to have his warm hand to hold.

I went home 20 pounds heavier, unable to sleep as my skin was so itchy, a reaction to the treatment. I scratched myself bloody. It took a few days for the fluid to go away. I spent my recovery time in flip flops and the baggiest pair of shorts I owned. It was June and a hot summer.

My mom and sister came out for the second week of treatments. Jolene and I had always been close. Her leukemia diagnosis changed our relationship during our teen years, but we remained tightly connected.

Now that I was going through a similarly dire diagnosis, our bond only strengthened. She and my mom took turns staying with me at the hospital, giving Alan a much needed break. Those few days with my mom and sister felt different, as if the darkness created a space for new light, allowing me to be more real and vulnerable with them and for them to be real with me.

A few days after they left, Alan and I planned to go to an outdoor concert. The temperatures were in the upper 90s, and the sun beat mercilessly on the parched grass. I felt like crap—sluggish, tired, and just drained. Not just from the cancer treatments, but from much of the activity we packed in while my mom and sister were in town. I really just wanted nothing more than to sit at home and do nothing.

But I also wanted to hear the band that was playing at our favorite outdoor concert venue. I grew to enjoy bluegrass and folk music, both as a child listening to good old-fashioned country, as well as in Indianapolis when I started seeking out small music venues during a brief relationship with a guitar-playing romantic. I had forgotten how much I enjoyed music and going to live concerts until I'd met him.

The band at that evening's concert came highly recommended by other friends who enjoyed similar music. I was really torn, but Alan convinced me to go. It would make me feel better, he said assuredly.

As we walked across the field to the shady grove with the stage area and open seating, I saw Jane, one of my coworkers, walking ahead of me. I was mortified and didn't want her to see me in my sorry state. My skin was blotchy, and my ankles were swollen. I did my best to stay far behind her and not make eye contact. The seating area was packed, more than any other night that we had visited this venue. We placed our chairs up at the end of the field and pulled out our wine, store-bought sandwiches, and salad. I looked around at the crowd to ensure that I was out of my coworker's line of sight.

The music started and I was soon lost in thoughts—I wondered if my coworker had spotted me and seen my pink blotches and cankles. I wondered if this would be my last summer concert. I fanned myself, cursed the heat, and marveled at the large crowd.

I tried to listen to the lyrics and pay attention to the band. They were good, and a few of their songs actually took me out of myself and transported me to the Blackjack Supper Club and dreaming of eating lots of Pie, the titles of two of their songs. The fiddle player had an amazing voice and talent for the instrument. The fiddle is my favorite instrument, and one I secretly wished I could play—instead of the boring clarinet I chose to master as a youngster.

I was enjoying the music. Alan and I didn't say much, as he held my hand, giving it occasional squeezes that I knew were code for I love you. I squeezed his back. We sipped our wine, glancing around at the larger than normal crowd. I kept looking where my coworker was sitting, hoping that she hadn't noticed me and wouldn't make a beeline to say hello. She seemed safely ensconced in conversation with the young couple with her. I felt bad that I didn't say hello, but I just couldn't bring myself to do so. I was fine with perfect strangers seeing my blotchy, bloated skin—they didn't know what I looked like on better days.

After an intermission, the band returned to the stage and the amazing fiddle player took the mic. Her voice was sweet and youthful. She thanked the crowd for coming and said she wanted to introduce her father, who was in the audience.

"He has stage four melanoma and was just declared cancer-free," she announced in her sweet voice.

Her words shot through me like an arrow. I didn't hear anything else she said as the meaning of her statement penetrated my worries about fat ankles, blotchy skin, and coworker sightings. I felt like I was the only person in the crowd. I saw the paper and my doctor's handwriting. Five to seven percent. *Cure.* The tail of the curve. Home runs. Those dreams became real.

I looked up and saw a giant of a man stand up and wave his ballcap in the air. He was smiling. Beaming in fact. His fair skin and light hair glowed in the late afternoon sun. He stood bathed in an aura of hope like an angel. Her announcement was biblical; the word was made flesh. The crowd clapped. I could see his smile as he turned to sit back down in his lawn chair. I turned to Alan and the tears welled in my eyes and rolled down my cheeks. I grabbed his hand and we held on tightly.

My mind raced and emotions tumbled over themselves. I felt disbelief at what I had just heard. A surge of hope raced through my veins and immediately lifted my heavy heart. I couldn't make sense of it. This man was a sign of hope I hadn't thought existed. His daughter's words giving proof to what I had thought was a hopeless pipe dream. Cancer-free? From stage four melanoma? Those five words didn't belong together. I could see flashes of "5% to 7%" on the piece of paper my doctor gave me with a list of treatments. Could those numbers be sitting in this crowd with me? Could there be some truth to the percentages? If there is, could there be two members of the 5 to 7 percent club in the same town, the same little park, listening to the same band?

I was beaming with hope but dreading the odds.

As the band wrapped up their set, I was an emotional basket case. People started packing up their picnic items and lawn chairs, and were filing their way out of the little grassy grove. I badly wanted to go seek out that giant dreamlike figure, to wrap my arms around him and thank him for giving me hope. I wanted to bow at his feet and put my melanoma fears in his hands. His miracle hands.

I struggled to gather up our belongings, not knowing what to say. I was sure that Alan would think I was crazy for wanting to talk to him. Neither of us said a word, as we carried our things toward the exit. I kept looking back to see if I could catch a glimpse of my angel, but I couldn't see him through the large crowd. I felt so torn. Part of me wanted to run back and find him. And the other part couldn't bring myself to make my legs move in that direction. I was embarrassed by my emotional state, and struggled to imagine what I would say if I did encounter him. He was cancer-free. I was cancer-full— the lumps still lurking underneath my skin.

We walked to the car in silence, both of us teary-eyed and bewildered as we left our hero to bask in his glory and newfound fans.

Two days after the concert an email appeared in my inbox. The subject line read: *Rochelle—you are in our thoughts and prayers—John.* My angel had a name, and it was John. Alan had sent a note to the band's manager who forwarded it to the fiddle player, who responded with a sweet note and gave Alan her father's email address. I was touched by Alan's gesture and nervously excited to tell my angel what I could not bring myself to say after the concert.

I typed out my email.

*Congratulations on being cancer-free! I am so glad you asked your daughter to make that announcement at the concert the other night. You are an inspiration to me and others who are battling this terrible disease.*

*I have been dreaming of the day when the doctor tells me I'm cancer-free, but have been reluctant to believe it is anything more than just a dream. Your experience makes me believe it is truly possible, and for that I am eternally grateful to you. Hope is a very powerful healing force, and you just gave me a huge dose. Interleukin may be serious stuff, but believing in a cure is the first step to being cured. Thank you for a renewed sense of hope.*

I didn't care if he responded, it was more my need to thank this superhuman figure who had just given me a gift that I'd never imagined receiving. To see his note, to read his words, was like reading my own journal entries. I read his note repeatedly, feeling a bond and connection that not even Alan could fulfill. John was speaking the same language I was learning. The language of life and death, hope and fear; words of wisdom and vulnerability that slip out naturally yet uncontrollably like how I imagine people who are so taken by the spirit that they speak in tongues. I felt heard and understood by a man who had typed such simple but profound thoughts.

I'd rejected the suggestions from others to find a support group or even search online for others facing my disease. The prognosis sounded so dire that it seemed pointless to reach out to or connect with others who would all be dead or dying. I didn't expect to find someone who survived long enough to be on the tail of the survival curve. To live longer than 6 months, much less be declared cancer-free. Yet, I'd found a person who was as hopeful as I wanted to be, and living as I wanted to live.

Seeing John validated my fantasies of surviving and my gut feeling that I'd live; the rush of hope that had shot through me when the doctor scribbled "cure" on the paper during our first visit. I lived that summer with intense joy and freedom, allowing myself to be more vulnerable and open than I'd ever been before. Yet, at the same time, I was determined to be the same person I always was. The active outdoors woman who hiked, biked, and ran. My best friends were the ones still inviting me to summit peaks and cycle hilly routes in the foothills. Others recognized when I needed quiet nights at home after the weeklong treatments, times when my body was bloated and blotchy.

In my darkest hour, facing my toughest challenge, the friendships that I'd been developing deepened and grew stronger. The wall I that I'd built around myself no longer served a purpose, so I stopped fighting to keep it intact. I began to experience the grace of undeserving favor and gratitude, for the gift of illness to help me clearly see and experience all the life around me.

# six

# Losing Grip

The first round of treatments was complete; two weeks in the hospital separated by a week at home. It was time to wait and see if I had hit a home run or swung and missed. In 6 weeks, I would get another scan to see if the protocol was working.

I needed some fresh air, and our go-to activity was to summit a peak where I could see for miles and miles and forget that I was dying. Given that I'd spent 2 of the last 3 weeks in the hospital, we decided to aim for a mountain pass instead of a peak, thinking it might be easier.

It was a gorgeous summer day—perfect for peak-bagging. Or pass-bagging, as it would have to be. Our wake-up alarm went off early, and we drove nearly 2 hours to the trailhead, hoping to snag one of the up-close parking spots. It was a popular place, and on weekends the lot filled up quickly.

I gazed out the car window as we drove along the winding highway through the canyon, the sun barely reaching the tree tops. The car was fully shaded by the high rock walls on either side. I couldn't wait to get out to breathe in the fresh pine-scented air and listen to the forest sounds. To go where I always feel better—into Mother Nature's arms.

The trail followed the edge of the lake in a thick ponderosa pine forest. I remembered the tree roots, as well as the logs and makeshift bridges over the marshy sections, which always threatened to trip me if I wasn't careful. We'd traveled this trail before to climb peaks and explore high alpine lakes. It was in one of the many beautiful wilderness areas within easy driving distance of Denver. This place, however, was more rugged and even more stunningly beautiful than the others with its smattering of lakes and jagged peaks.

I felt the comfort of a known trail and the embrace of the wooded and mostly silent path as we walked along. Similar to our days in Bryce Canyon right after the doctor's call, my senses clued into details that I had never noticed before. Like the little pool of water shimmering in the morning sun. Or the number of dead trees and hollowed logs strewn about the forest floor. And the flying insects and crawling bugs, were they always there? I stayed in Bryce mode and tried to capture as many mental pictures as possible—to see as much as I could in that shaded forest. A forest I'd traveled before, but was seeing again for the first time.

And now all these firsts felt like they could potentially be my lasts as well.

My legs weren't their strongest, but my ankles had reverted to normal size, and my feet were happy to be back in hiking boots and out of the flip flops that had been the only home lately for my swollen toes. I took my normal lead position, but I could tell I was walking more slowly than usual as Alan stayed right on my heels. I should've just let him go ahead, but I couldn't. I didn't want to lag behind or exhibit another sign of my weak and failing body.

"Do you want to pass me?" I asked, hoping he'd say yes. And no.

"No, you're fine."

I wished that were true—that I was fine. A fine hiker. A fine pacesetter. A fine fiancée. Anything fine. I wanted to be fine. But I knew I was not.

My favorite part of hiking mountains is that feeling of freedom you have when you are above the tree line and no longer hemmed in by the forest. After nearly 2 miles of shaded trail, we finally left the trees as the trail switchbacked up, then crossed a creek and looked out into a glacial basin with a shimmering ice-blue lake. We stopped to admire the sparkling water and jagged peaks encircling the basin.

We weren't quite halfway to the pass, and I knew the trail only would become steeper and rockier. I wasn't feeling bad, and if we were normal weekend warriors this beautiful lake would've been our turnaround point. But we were not typical weekend warriors, escaping our urban commotion for a similar crowd at an alpine lake.

We had higher aspirations. I took some deep breaths and snapped photos with my mind's camera and pressed on.

Slowly.

I trudged up the first steep section along the creek, until it leveled a little before the trail followed along the ridge, zigzagging up the rocky cliffs and around big boulders. My steps became shorter, and my pace even slower. My legs felt like heavy wooden logs, as I kept my eyes on the ground to avoid tripping and the reality that I was getting nowhere. I felt bad for slowing us down, and kept asking Alan to pass me. Normally, I was the one to set the pace, but in the last few months I'd found myself walking behind Alan as I plodded along, trying to keep up with him. It was a clear sign that I was sick.

He finally gave in to my request and walked ahead of me. I kept placing one foot in front of the other, determined to keep up. I would get to the pass, dammit. I can't *not* make it. I watched as Alan seemed to move faster, and the distance between us grew larger. He glanced back every so often, and I'd give him a little thumbs up or head nod to assure that I was OK. But I had to keep stopping to catch my breath.

I looked ahead at the trail as it snaked its way up the mountainside above me to the right. I could see our destination, a V-shaped saddle between two rocky peaks. It didn't seem that far away. I put my head down and focused on taking one step at a time. After what seemed like hours, I looked up, expecting to be closer to the saddle, but the trail seemed to grow longer as more switchbacks appeared. I leaned on my hiking poles for a minute to catch my breath, and kept repeating, *One step at a time,* over and over. Instead of feeling better, I only felt worse.

My legs wouldn't move. My heart thumped in my chest as my lungs heaved. There simply wasn't enough oxygen in the universe to catch my breath. My head wanted to go on, but my body just slumped. Every step taken had felt like a mile. I glanced up ahead to see Alan's bright orange shirt a few switchbacks ahead, nearing the top of the steep slope. He didn't see me, and I hoped he wouldn't look down and see how far behind I was. I just needed to sit down.

I found a nice flat rock along the trailside and dropped heavily onto it, my chest still heaving, trying to find air. I wanted to scream, but my lungs couldn't summon enough oxygen to mutter a sound. Just silent sobs, angry swells. I couldn't even enjoy the trail's sheer beauty; my physical pain and exhaustion clouded the horizon. All I could see were peaks I couldn't climb. The air I couldn't seem to breathe. The fiancé I could no longer keep up with. And the vision of my body filled with cancer cells.

Placing my head in my lap, I cried hot angry tears and stared at the rocks between my feet. I don't know how long I sat there, but soon I felt a hand on my shoulder. Alan leaned over me, my body rising and falling with the sobs. He said, "We're turning around."

Leaning down to my level, he held me tightly as tears flowed onto his shoulder. "Let it go," he whispered in my ear.

I cried until the dry mountain air absorbed all my tears' salty sad moisture. I finally looked up and over at the ring of peaks before me and the sliver of blue lake peeking out at their base. I wasn't sure if I'd ever see this sight again. Terrified this would be my last time to feel the freedom of treeless slopes and rugged mountains all around me. Petrified it meant that I was losing my soul before losing my life.

I was crushed, my spirit deflated. I knew he was right. I had to turn around. I had to give up and give in to my weakening body. As I shuffled down the trail, the 4 miles dragged onward, my heavy legs barely leaving the ground. I wanted to apologize, but couldn't find a way to say I was sorry for dying. Nor could I fully accept my failing strength. No words came. I dejectedly tossed my pack into the car's backseat and climbed into then slumped into the passenger seat. Alan looked at me as we extended our arms to hold each other and cried.

We knew this could be my last hike. The next scan would confirm those fears or give me hope that my heart would experience another mountain summit.

---

A few weeks later, we sat in the doctor's examination room, anxiously awaiting the news. I sat on the exam table, and the doctor asked about my lumps. I couldn't feel them anymore.

"Really?" he responded, sliding his hands along my back. "Not even the big one that was here?" as he pressed down on the right side of my spine.

"Nope."

"Your scans show significant improvement," he commented. "The tumors are shrinking, and some have disappeared. And the lumps—that is a great sign."

I looked at Alan, a smile forming on my face. Hope arrived. My body had responded to the treatment. Maybe I just hit my home run. He smiled back, and we spent the rest of the appointment planning for the next round of treatments.

The results arrived just before our trip to Iowa for a family wedding. Thankfully, I could show up with happy news, rather than endure the walking funeral I had imagined.

I went home and sent an email to my angel, John, telling him of my "significant improvement." He sent back a message of congratulations, noting the word significant. "That sounds like really good news," he wrote. "You've won a ticket to another round!"

We exchanged a few more emails, sharing details of the treatment and commiserating over side effects. The words flowed effortlessly, as if we had known each other for years, not mere months, and through a couple of email notes. He understood the deeper meaning of those results, and I could feel his shared joy.

We made it through the summer and more weeks of treatment. The crisp fall air and sharp blue skies of autumn brought renewed hope. The sun streamed through the sliding glass doors as I sat at the kitchen table with my laptop, trying to respond to work emails and finish up a few tasks before I left for my next scan. I couldn't concentrate—all my mind wanted to think about was the next scan. *Could it be clean? Free of tumors?* Only a few spots were left on my spleen and liver. This could be the best birthday present ever. It could mean the last round of treatment is already complete. Maybe I wouldn't have to return for another two weeks of bloating, fever, and unconscious Demerol-induced sleep.

Yet, I worried about my slurred speech and exhaustion. My face was still puffy, and my tongue so swollen it pushed against my teeth and I constantly bit the sides of my mouth. When I talked, it sounded like I'd had guzzled a couple shots of whiskey. My head throbbed, and waves of nausea washed over me as I tapped out messages. I hadn't felt this bad at any point in this process. Usually by this time in the IL-2 treatment, I would feel better, recovering and releasing all the water gain and swollenness. Paranoia crept back like a blanket being pulled over my eyes. I'd been frantically scanning my back and arms before dressing for work in the morning, and again at night before I went to bed, praying I wouldn't feel any new lumps. I hoped I only had a stress headache, and not a tumor in my brain.

I worried about driving 30 minutes on the highway when I felt I could pass out at any moment. I tried to convince myself it was the fasting before the scan; I told myself I merely had low blood sugar.

I watched the clock as the time for my departure approached, partly wishing it would go faster and half-hoping it would stand still. I didn't know what to do. I had to do this scan. It was my birthday scan. We were going on a weekend trip to celebrate a birthday I hadn't been sure I'd live to see. My fortieth. I thought it would be great to turn 40 cancer-free.

I closed my laptop and grabbed my keys from the counter. The little "Thinking of You" card poked out from under the stack of junk mail. I reread the handwritten note, wondering how this person knew I needed her message at that moment. I smiled, pulling the card to my chest. I stopped to snuggle with my pooch before I left, telling him I hoped to make it through this. His big brown eyes looked back at me, begging me to stay. I wished I could just curl up with him on the couch and let my dizziness fade into the cushions.

I stayed in the right lane on the interstate in case I needed to quickly exit or if I felt like I was going to pass out. I felt like an old lady with a white-knuckle grip on the steering wheel, following the speed limit as I over-concentrated on staying between the white lines. I breathed a huge sigh of relief when I finally reached my exit, and could leave the racecar drivers behind.

I walked into the facility, grabbing the handrail along the wall, and carefully walked to the waiting area to check in. I was a wee early, so I took a seat in the row of chairs along the wall and leaned my head back. My nausea and lightheadedness returned with hot flashes and sweats, my vision blurring slightly, reminding me of a time when I had fainted in our farmhouse kitchen. I placed my head between my legs and hoped the feeling would go away before the tech came to retrieve me. I imagined this feeling happening while strapped inside the scanning device. The thought made the nausea even worse. Closing my eyes, I tried to calm my mind, focusing on my breath. All my meditative tricks were useless, as my breath only quickened and my heartbeat like a rock-and-roll drummer in my chest. *It's all mental,* I told myself. *I'm psyching myself out.*

Nothing worked.

Through my mind's chattering, I heard my name called. I lifted my head to see the cute young tech with his broad smile. My legs felt like lead as I pushed myself up from the chair and walked toward him.

"How are you doing?" he asked.

"Well, not that great, to be honest."

He asked for details. I told him my symptoms and tried to reassure him with all my rationalizations of low blood sugar, the water weight gain, and normal puffiness. I wasn't sure if I was trying to convince him—or myself.

He listened and nodded, his expression not revealing any clues as to whether this was normal, or if I could still do the scan. I wished he'd tell me what to do.

"Do you want to postpone? We can do that. I'll be here tomorrow afternoon, but you need to decide now. The radioactive dye we use has a short shelf life."

I was so torn between the imagined birthday celebration and the image of me puking in the PET scan tube. *Oh shit,* I thought. *Alan will kill me. We're supposed to leave tomorrow after the doctor appointment. Now, I won't have the scan before the appointment, and it is all messed up.* I couldn't figure out what was going on with my body. Rage rose upward from my gut and mixed with nausea. I couldn't tell which was winning.

"I must know in the next 5 minutes," the tech added.

Panic overwhelmed me, and I didn't know what to do. There simply was no time to call Alan for advice. No time to make any of this go away.

"I'm so sorry. I'm going to have to come back." I couldn't go in that tube feeling like that. And I could potentially waste some precious radioactive material specifically measured for me. I would not only fail myself, but now I felt I was failing the tech too. As if the vial of liquid and his duty to administer it were measures of my worth.

"OK, That's fine," he replied. "I'll put you down for tomorrow. I hope you feel better."

I merely nodded as I dropped my head and walked past the receptionist who gave me a "What-are-you-doing" look? I said nothing, but found the same handrail that guided me into the building and walked back out.

I sat in my car for a long time, cussing and slapping the steering wheel. I cursed myself for not being able to endure 45 minutes in the tube, and for ruining our grand birthday plans. All I could think about was, *how I was going to tell Alan? He's going to be mad.*

I pulled into my usual parking space in front of his door, and took a deep breath as I walked up the steps.

"What are you doing here so early?" he asked as he opened the door.

"I couldn't do it. I feel like shit, and I thought I was going to puke or pass out." I rattled off my crappy symptoms and rationalizations to convince him that I really felt like crap, and that I really couldn't do it. I hoped he didn't think I was making it up. I wanted him to believe me. I didn't want him to think I was a quitter.

He didn't say much, and I knew enough not to press the issue. We sat on the couch in the now-familiar awkward silence, also known as disappointment, whose real name is fear. I sat in a pool of pity and self-hatred, and growing angrier at my decision to forego the scan.

*I'm just a quitter*, I thought. *Have been all my life.* I quit band in high school even though I was first chair. I quit playing basketball even though I became a starter in my first year in college. I quit numerous jobs to take other positions that I thought were better. I quit running the last six miles of my marathon and let myself settle for less than my Boston qualifying goal. And here I am quitting again as I get to the finish line. My failures washed over me like a crushing wave. *I'm a loser.* I worried that Alan would see me as a failure, a fake, a fraud. I couldn't handle this stupid scan and assumed we would have to forego our weekend away.

I couldn't take the silence any longer, and all my thoughts spewed out as I apologized for ruining our plans, for being a terrible girlfriend, a weak woman who can't even handle a little nausea. I blurted out all my quitting failures as hot angry tears rolled down my face. I told him he could still leave me. We weren't married yet.

I couldn't stop my flow of rage, the well so deep I was afraid I'd never stop crying. All my past mistakes burying me in those familiar feelings of failure. I couldn't even do *this* right. I couldn't even succeed as a cancer patient. *What the fuck!* I cussed and cursed myself, blubbering into my hands as I tried to cover my eyes and shield Alan from seeing what a sobbing hot mess I was. I felt him get up from the couch, assuming I had gotten my wish. That he was walking away. I clenched my eyes tighter.

Suddenly, his hands grabbed my shoulders, and he pulled me up from the couch, squeezing so hard I was afraid my bones would pop. He demanded that I stand on his coffee table. I thought he was losing his mind. I stared at him in disbelief while he kept insisting.

He pushed aside the magazines and drink coasters, "Stand up on the coffee table. Now."

I was so delirious with my own anxiety that I couldn't even fight back. He hoisted me up on the narrow wood slab and told me to "stay" like a dog in training. I watched as he went upstairs, feeling like a fool left standing on his sleek table. I couldn't imagine what he was doing.

A few seconds later, I heard footsteps, and he walked down the stairs; one arm tucked behind his back. He stood in front of me, his head now at my shoulders as he looked up at me and into my tear-swollen eyes.

"You are a champion. You are a fighter. You are alive. You are the toughest woman I know. And I love you." He brought his arm around and in his hand was one of his golden swimming medals. He reached up and placed the ribbon around my neck. He made me repeat what he said. *I am a champion. I am a fighter. I am alive. I am the toughest woman.*

I nodded; my mouth was not able to form the words.

"Look at me and say it."

He was serious.

I looked down at him and our eyes locked. Through tears I stammered out the words and fell into his arms.

---

Two days later, we met with the doctor and got the scan results. Spots remained, and I would need another round of treatment. We still took our trip to the mountains and summited a 13,000-foot peak to celebrate my birthday and another step closer to the finish line. And a week later, tests revealed the cause of my swollen tongue and lingering symptoms. The treatment had wrecked my thyroid. One nurse wondered how I even got out of bed when she saw my numbers.

*seven*

---

# Leveling Off

Long before I arrived, the organization had always appointed one staff member who acted as a de facto director to cover for my boss while he was off being brilliant and charming with the rest of the world. This role was as close to having his job as I could get, and I'd wanted my boss's job since I had first began working for him. I believed he had the best position, because he knew all the national experts and worked with influential movers and shakers from across the country.

My first business trip with him to the Arkansas capitol, I watched as he deftly networked. He seemed to know everyone, and everyone knew him. Some didn't like him because he wasn't on their side; he always made it clear whose back he had, and that he'd do whatever they asked of him.

I wanted that prestige and to be renowned as an expert. People in the industry knew his name and his brilliance. He could rattle off facts about every state in the union without hesitation. But what he didn't really enjoy was management. It wasn't a secret, but something that the organization chose to tolerate as I had been warned about in my interview. I agreed to abide by their indifference, despite the stress and strain on the rest of his team. When the de facto director left, I volunteered to take on the role.

"Well, ok, if you want to give it a try, we can try," was my boss's response when I told him I wanted the position.

There was enough doubt in his voice to fan the flames of doubt even higher. I wanted to prove to him that I could do it. And that I could be better than any of his previous deputies.

Like the brief fad of WWJD, or "what would Jesus do," I swapped my boss's name for "Jesus"—what would Jack do? When people came to me asking about his work, inquiring where was this report, what was the budget for this project, why wasn't this done on time, etc., I'd switch into boss mode and answer as if I were him. When he was being criticized, I played myself, using my super people-pleasing powers to smooth over any rough spots and bend over backwards to make things right.

I found myself in a constant internal tug-of-war between what *I* would do, and what *he* would do. I defended actions that I found disrespectful and covered up his missed deadlines and undelivered projects. I often didn't know what task he neglected or botched would come across my desk. With a mixture of pride and resentment, I fulfilled my deputy duties and coined a new title for myself: Chief Cat Herder and Ego Stroker.

My boss never said anything more about my role after I raised my hand for the job, and we slid into our new dance steps rather easily.

More than a year into my deputy role, a coworker knocked on my office door. "The boss is in the hospital," she whispered. "They think he has cancer."

My mind raced as I thought about all the work I would be required to do if he was out of the office and even more unreachable than our usual sporadic phone calls. A quick Google search gave a dire prognosis for his type of cancer; the average survival was two to three years. I could hardly believe what I was reading. He'd been a stalwart in the industry for years. He wasn't even 60 years old. He had two young sons. I felt so sorry for him.

Yet, in the back of my mind, I secretly wondered if this meant I could have his job in 2 to 3 years. I imagined being fully in charge and leading the department *my* way, not constantly trying to figure out what I thought he wanted me to do. I could feel the freedom that it would give me. My Catholic guilt quickly jerked me out of that daydream as I hushed and tried to ignore that dream.

I doubled-down on my role as his de factor director, attending his meetings and following up on his phone calls. Playing supportive cheerleader when he was feeling down, I wrote a weekly newsletter summarizing the office happenings with tidbits from the staff. I did everything in my power to keep things running smoothly. His longer-than-normal absence revealed new problems; I added "firefighter" to my title.

The double duty was wearing on my patience and stamina. My thick skin stretched every time I faced backlash or blame for something he was supposed to do. I'd been trying to detach from my job and deal with the stress of my role, shutting off my phone, not checking emails, and doing everything I could to recharge on weekends so I could go back and do it all over again on Monday. I felt like Kevin Bacon in Animal House, *Thank you, sir, may I have another*.

I definitely got another. Less than a year after his diagnosis, I received the biopsy results of my lump showing metastatic melanoma with an average 9-month survival rate. The gods were mocking me.

I felt terrible guilt about having wanted his job and wondering whether his illness would be my opportunity to advance. I could see a judgmental figure in the sky, wagging his finger at me, and calling me a greedy little bitch, telling me to try on stage four cancer for myself.

It felt like a cruel punishment for my evil thoughts—and a ticket to freedom. Freedom from the "what would the boss do" syndrome. I didn't care if I got his job. Hell, I would probably die before him. Talk about irony. I had worked to cover his ass and whose butt gets kicked to the curb? While he was in remission, I went off to battle the cancer dogs with the odds stacked squarely against me. I assumed I'd beat him to the grave.

I refused to work during the four-week treatment cycles; I'd be in the hospital for one week, out for one, back in for another round, and then out again. I had bigger battles to fight than all the piddly fires and politicking I'd been doing. Since my boss was feeling better, he promised to fill in for me. And I believed he would.

That is, until he didn't. The one deadline I needed him to meet, he totally ignored.

I laughed at his oversight, instead of rushing to save the situation. All the time that I'd spent covering up for him; listening to people whine, complain, and even yell at me for his work, I almost hoped someone was yelling at him about me. Sometimes, I believed in karma.

---

The beauty of being on death's doorstep meant not caring one bit about work. My job finally fell off its pedestal and landed with a thud. Or maybe it landed without any sound at all, it went away so easily. I thought my first cancer diagnosis had given me freedom to not worry about the small stuff—but this diagnosis took away all worries, large and small.

My singular focus on living seemed to be working. I responded to the treatments, and it looked like I might live to see my 40s. My boss's boss approached me near the end of my treatments, as I was planning my full-time return to the office.

"We'd like to promote you to your boss's position." He looked at me expectantly.

"What does that mean for him?"

"You would supervise him."

I resisted the urge to slap him in the face, and instead just flatly responded, "No."

His eyes bugged out of his head as if I'd just announced I was an alien from another planet. Which, in some ways, I was. In the past, I had said yes to anything the company asked of me. Now they were handing me my dream job, which I had refused. I would no longer abide by their tolerance of disrespectful behavior and be left to clean up a mess they allowed to fester for years. I told him as much, but he didn't change the terms of the offer.

"Think about it," he said, assuming I just needed some time to come to my senses. Adding he needed a final answer the next day.

He returned the next day, and my answer remained a firm refusal.

They announced the position change for my boss and posted the job. I knew an internal candidate who would apply. I had no idea what kind of resumes might come from the outside. This level of position rarely opened. It was my dream job. I knew I could do it. I wanted to do it. I succumbed to my ego—and the fear of getting an even worse boss—and sent in my resume an hour before the deadline.

Heck, I'd just kicked cancer's ass; I figured I'd just keep kicking.

My interview was scheduled for a few days after completing my last week of treatments. I wore my favorite jacket, did my best to style my straggly thin hair, and desperately tried to put some color in my face with a powder foundation. With nothing to lose, I strode confidently into the windowless office where they were holding the interviews and shook everyone's hands. I sat straight in my chair, answering all their questions easily, even the veiled attempts to gauge what I would do about my boss and his difficult behavior. They smiled and nodded, and seemed pleased with my answers. As we closed the interview, I thanked them for the opportunity and their support.

Part of me started planning the first months of my new position. What I would do and how I'd handle the awkward role of becoming my boss's boss. The other part imagined walking away from the office and never looking back. Regardless of the outcome, I would win.

The next day I stood in the shower after a hard workout, tipping my head back and enabling the warm water and salty sweat to run down my back. I grabbed the loofah and soap and began scrubbing my arms, when I noticed my right arm was a deep red from my bicep down to my fingertips. As I ran my fingers along this scarlet patch, I felt a tingling sensation as if I'd just hit my funny bone. My other arm was pale white as usual. I wasn't sure what to think, but it didn't really hurt, so I let it go, assuming the redness would fade away.

The next day my arm was a much darker red. Worry and panic flooded my thoughts. I called the doctor, and she immediately ordered an ultrasound. It is probably a blood clot, she explained.

My brain immediately traveled back years ago to my mom telling me that my dad was in the hospital with a blood clot, which started in his leg and had traveled to his lung. Then me calling my aunt, a nurse, asking if I should come home. Her advice was, "I can't tell you what to do, but this is serious." If my aunt says it's serious, then it must be. I was on a flight in no time.

I was just a few days out from cancer treatments, having completed 6 weeks in the hospital for intensive treatments over the course of 6 months, my PET scans were nearly cancer-free, and now I faced a new battle—blood clots in my arm.

As I laid on the exam table, the ultrasound tech put a slimy goo on my arm, and moved the ultrasound wand over my bicep and inner arm, and confirmed the diagnosis. There were multiple clots. I had to go straight up to the 12th floor to my oncologist.

I was seething mad. So angry. And tired. Trying to make sense of what it meant. I imagined blood thinners, bruises, and tiny cuts turning into raging red rivers. And I recalled that pulmonary embolism episode with my dad. I worried the clots in my arm would go to my lungs and kill me.

My doctor was very calm and nonchalant about the whole thing. "The PICC lines surely caused this. It can be a side effect. Get this medicine at the pharmacy, then come back here. The nurse will show you how to give yourself the injections."

Injections? I've been poked and prodded; given more Demerol than is legal; had sleepless nights, puking fits, and diarrhea. I was finally done with all that, and now I had to give myself shots?

I thought I had beaten cancer. I thought I was done with the poking and prodding. I thought I was getting back to normal. I certainly didn't want to inflict pain with my own hands.

My frustration at having to endure another three months of shots and medical hell quickly manifested through tears that fell from my eyes. My doctor didn't know what to do with her normally upbeat patient. I hadn't cried in front of her throughout this whole ordeal.

"Why are you crying? It's going to be OK. This is easy. You just survived IL-2. That is like war. This is a piece of cake."

"I know. I'm fine." I blubbered. "I'm just tired."

She wrapped her arms around me and told me it was going to be OK. I let her envelop me as I choked back the tears, remembering what she said. *This is a piece of cake. The hard work is over.*

I sat in the pharmacy waiting area for my box of syringes, alcohol swabs, and vials of medicine. Across from me was a wall of over-the-counter drugs—acetaminophen, ibuprofen, bandages of every size, antibiotic creams, and antacids. I stared across the room blinking back tears. I was exhausted—sick of needles, IVs, heart monitors, painkillers, and just doctors in general.

The memory of the past 6 months rushed over me and wiped me out. I felt paralyzed—the weight of my reality crushing my shoulders. I looked around for a corner or somewhere to curl up and cry. I just wanted to bawl my eyes out in private.

My self-pitying thoughts were suddenly interrupted by my cell phone ringing. The name showed up on my caller ID—my boss's boss. I was suddenly brought back to that other reality and remembered my interview.

Walking out into the hallway, I pulled the phone to my ear. "Hello, this is Rochelle." hoping my voice sounded normal.

"Rochelle, how are you?'

"I'm fine," I said, lying through my teeth.

"I want to offer you the director position. Starting December 1st." He rattled off other particulars as I stood trying to comprehend it all. "What do you think?"

I watched a woman walk by pushing an IV pole, wearing a pink fuzzy hat, and closed my eyes. The juxtaposition of illness and dream jobs was another ironic metaphor of my life in that moment. I thought about putting him off until the next day, but instead I mumbled, "I guess I'll take it."

"I'm really glad you decided to do this. You'll be great. Thanks, and have a good night."

I hung up the phone and stood in disbelief at what was happening. I walked back over to my chair in the waiting room, sat down and put my hands over my face, shaking my head.

Five minutes later, I sat in the chemo room with my bag of goodies from the pharmacy. A very kind nurse explained how to use everything, and showed me where to give myself shots in the stomach. A stomach churning with nerves. I lifted my shirt and unbuttoned my pants as she explained how to pinch my belly fat around my navel and push the needle into the fold of skin.

I thanked her for all her help and grabbed up my bags of needles, alcohol swabs, and the phone number for the blood-clot clinic. I walked out into the now-darkened street where the cool air hit my face and sent a shiver through my body. I looked up at the sky, searching for stars, as the black expanse swallowed me into its darkness. The tears I held back earlier came flooding down my cheeks. My shoulders shook as I walked to the car, clutching my big plastic bag of medical supplies. Tossing it on the passenger seat, I rested my head on the steering wheel, and cried a cocktail of tears. A big shot of exhaustion, an ounce or two of anger, and a mere splash of relief.

I texted Alan to let him know I was finally on my way home. The streets were blurry; my tears made it feel like I was like driving through a rainstorm.

## eight

# Celebrating

I took over the position as director on December 1st. I was still giving myself shots and getting daily blood draws, but I was, I hoped, finished with the treatments. Nearly 2 weeks later, on Friday the 13th, Alan and I sat in our usual positions in the mauve-colored vinyl chairs in the exam room. I sat by the doctor's desk with Alan to my right. Our hands interlocked with the occasional squeeze, as we sat in silence staring at the sterile walls and the same poster describing the various stages of melanoma.

We'd survived six rounds of IL-2, and I had my latest PET scan a few days ago. We were hoping that it was finally clean. We had been so close in September— just a few spots had shown up on my spleen. I hoped they were gone. I didn't think I could endure another round of 2 weeks in the hospital, followed by 6 weeks of waiting. The last week of treatment nearly did me in. The nausea and diarrhea had been noticeably worse, and I had clutched the blue barf bag close to my face for the entire car ride home. My hair was starting to fall out, and I looked pale and sickly. All my pigment was gone, except a few spots on my knuckles. Otherwise, I was white as chalk. I hoped we were out of the eye of the storm, and that things were going to calm down—but it *was* Friday the 13th.

I remembered the receptionist reciting the date and time back to me on the phone, and I cringed at the realization. Not wanting to wait until the following week for the results, I agreed to the appointment time and ignored the black cat bad news images flashing before me. The date seemed to match the irony that I was even alive. Not much in my life made much sense or followed a normal pattern anymore, so why not find out if I'm free of cancer on Friday the 13th?

I am crazy superstitious. In high school, I wore the same socks, underwear, and bra for basketball and softball games, following strict rituals and never straying from my routine. I don't like black cats or sidewalk cracks. I fret over broken mirrors. Friday the 13th always added a little extra fear and caution, as I would go through that day cautiously to avoid messing with the bad-luck gods.

We heard the familiar knock, and the doctor opened the door, looked at both of us, glanced at our clenched hands and anxious faces, and a smile began to spread across his face.

"The scans are clear," he proudly announced as he shut the door behind him.

Oh my gosh. I looked over at Alan and we hugged. I could hardly sit still—I wanted to jump up and down and scream *Hallelujah, Amen,* or *Hell Yes*! Joy and relief surged through my system, threatening to bust out of my pores like a geyser as I smiled and squeezed Alan's hand, looking back at him and at the doctor again. I wanted to high-five, scream, and hug, as I'd have done after winning a basketball game.

The doctor excitedly pulled up the scans on his computer screen. We scrolled through my whole body, scouring the black-and-gray images for those familiar pinkish-white spots—the tumors that had dotted the screen for so many months.

Nothing.

Scrolling back and forth over the trouble areas, he pointed out the places that had had tumors, and then compared them to the first scan. The images looked to be from a different person. The spots on my liver were gone. My spine was just bones—no tumors. And the last spots on my spleen now simply grayish-black blobs.

On our first visit, I wasn't sure my doctor even had the ability to smile, wondering if his cheek muscles had atrophied over the years of dealing with stage-four melanoma cases. The average survival was 9 months when I had been diagnosed, and I knew he had lost many patients. Perhaps his face lost the muscle memory to smile at good news, having so few opportunities to deliver positive messages to his patients. I can still see his serious and calm face as he told us that the treatments probably wouldn't work, but this was our only shot at a home run. He knew the numbers and openly shared the statistics.

"Let's go look at them on the big screen."

He escorted us to their computer room where two large monitors sat side by side on a table. He pulled up a chair for me and Alan stood behind me, as the doctor logged in and found my file with the latest images. He put the first scan on the left screen, and this fourth and most recent scan on the right. I couldn't believe the difference between them, with the scan on the right without those pink spots dotting my body just 7 months before.

I wriggled in my chair like a 5-year-old who had eaten too much sugar—my giddiness coursing through my veins. The doctor excitedly talked about my body's transformation and my full response. I felt like a prize fighter and almost expected him to raise up my arm in victory. I wanted to throw my arms around him like an athlete hugging their coach after winning the gold medal. I kept glancing over my shoulder at Alan, incredulous and thrilled, amazed and so grateful. He beamed and stood in awe of the images on the screens.

The doctor stood up and gestured for us to follow him. He took us further down the hall to what I could tell were the nurse and other offices. We entered a room on the right where at least six other doctors and nurses were gathered.

"This is my full-response patient," he beamed.

They looked at me with big smiles spreading on their faces and clapped. I was on parade. The master of ceremonies. The Tony-award winner. I was a champion. He was showing me off like a celebrity. I blushed at their congratulations and kind words. I had to thank him. I had to give my acceptance speech.

"Can I give you a hug?" I asked our usually brusque doctor who turned beaming like a proud miracle worker.

I didn't even wait for a response and wholeheartedly wrapped my arms around his waist and squeezed hard.

"Thank you," I said, looking up at him with admiration, respect, and pure joy.

He awkwardly put his arms around me, clearly surprised by my frontal attack. I could sense that the nurses and doctors were surprised as well, not just by my enthusiasm but that someone hugged the doctor. In front of them. I didn't care if I broke some sort of doctor-patient boundary. This man saved my life for crying out loud. He deserved way more than a hug. We stood among the admiring fans, and the doctor rattled off all the relevant statistics. They kept nodding and smiling.

We walked back to the exam room; the doctor still wanted to check me over. He noticed my pale skin with its few blotches of brown. Vitiligo like Michael Jackson, he explained. And he noticed my white eyelashes and another smile ripped across his face. Really, you're smiling at my white eyelashes? They're hideous. Not to mention the eyebrows, which now resemble those furry caterpillars, but instead of brown and black they are black and white.

He kept looking at my skin and the white hairs.

"This is a great sign."

I thought he was crazy.

"Can I take a picture of your eyelashes, so I can show my students?"

Enjoying this foray into what a happy doctor visit feels like, I just laughed and closed my eyes. Alan snickered from his chair and pulled out his phone.

"Check this out. Twins," he said while showing the screen to the doctor.

The two shared a belly laugh I had never thought possible when 7 months earlier the doctor was the gloom-and-doom Grim Reaper, and Alan scared and anxious. I couldn't imagine what was on Alan's screen, but he turned the phone towards me. My 10-year-old beagle stared back at me—through his white eyelashes. I now looked like my elderly dog.

I never thought I'd see my doctor smile and laugh, especially given his personal label as "the plague doctor." Alan and I floated out of the building, our hands entwined, and arms swinging like school children returning from a day on the playground. We walked into the bright daylight, our smiles outshining the big ball in the sky.

"I do believe it's happy hour."

A martini never tasted so good.

---

We threw a big New Year's Eve party and celebrated the wild ride that was 2013. I hadn't been sure that I would make it through the summer. Yet here it was, a frigid winter night with all our friends crammed into our little house, drinking, and laughing. The smile on my face was so wide my cheeks hurt. The evening was filled with numerous hugs and shots of tequila.

Life settled into a new rhythm, as I enjoyed my new role and freedom at work. Weekends were filled with mountain adventures, and everything paced along smoothly. We decided to go ahead and plan a wedding for later in the year, believing that we were out of the woods, and I was going to live to be a bride, not just a fiancée.

John, my dear angel on this journey whom we'd seen at the concert, and I had exchanged emails throughout the summer as I updated him on my progress and shared my scanxiety, the inevitable angst that occurred before every scan to see if the tumors had changed. He could relate to my experiences in a way that brought comfort and some normalcy to what sometimes felt like madness. I was so grateful for his openness and candor, and for his way with words. After my miraculous Friday the 13th cancer-free milestone, I sent a joyful note to share my news and wished him a happy new year. He responded with a simple, "That is great news. Happiest new year."

Never in our communication was he short on words. I knew something was wrong, but I heard nothing more until a month later, when we saw John's daughter and her band again. His daughter relayed the heavy news that his cancer had returned. I was devastated. The tables had turned. I was now cancer-free, yet he was returning to the hospital for more treatment. I reached out in hopes of offering the same inspiration he gave me. Our emails continued, as he kept me apprised of his progress and treatment steps.

It was January 2014. I was back in Iowa for my grandmother's funeral, feeling healthy again after achieving my cancer-free milestone.

"Would you like to try on my wedding dress?" my mother asked, as we sat around the kitchen table after the services.

I gulped, not anticipating her question or offer. "You think it would fit? Where is it?"

"In the attic. Of all the girls, you might be the only one it would fit," she laughed.

I didn't want to disappoint her, either by refusing to try it on or not choosing it as my dress. I kept picturing my parents' wedding photo on their tall dresser, and the dress's billowing train and long sleeves. I was sure it would be too elaborate for my simple style.

"It should be in a big suitcase on the right," my mom said, peering up at me as I climbed the attic's wooden ladder.

I hadn't been up there in years, not since they replaced the roof. Piles of insulation dotted the dusty floorboards. I saw the familiar boxes and tin Schwann's ice cream buckets full of papers that lined the far wall. I grabbed the suitcase and brought it over to the opening, and carefully handed it down to my sister. All five of us sisters were at the farm that night, having returned following my grandmother's services.

"Try it on," everyone cheered.

I opened the metal latches on the old hardbacked case, pulled out the crinkled plastic garment bag, carefully unzipped the bag, and pulled the rumpled white dress out of its covering. The material was bulky and wrinkled from being crammed into the suitcase for 47 years.

"It's probably pretty dirty. I never had it cleaned, and you know back then we wore a wedding dress all day. I remember the train getting pretty dusty."

My sisters grabbed the train and inspected its edges. The dress certainly saw a good party, as evidenced by the frayed brown edges. I figured it wasn't salvageable, but they unzipped the bodice and handed it to me, and I slid it up towards my hips and wriggled it over my butt.

"Mom, you were a rail when you got married! I can barely fit into this."

"I know. But I thought it might fit your skinny little body."

I slipped my arms into the long sleeves, and she zipped me up. "It fits perfectly," she exclaimed.

I looked at myself in the mirror, the straight-line dress hugging my slim waist. The simple lace bodice adding a slight feminine touch to the otherwise plain garment. It was exactly what I imagined—once I could imagine myself wearing a wedding gown. I had never thought my mother's dress would fit me so perfectly or be as simple and elegant as I wanted.

I looked at my mother and said, "I think I found my dress."

She and my sisters whooped with delight, clapping their hands and nodding.

"It is perfect."

Months later I went to the tailor shop to check on the dress's progress. I smiled as I twirled myself around, my casual leather sandals poking out from below the hem.

"This is perfect," I told the seamstress, who'd spent hours fixing the 1960's dress.

She beamed back at me. "You are so beautiful," she crooned.

I thanked her profusely and we hugged like we were long-lost friends. I had found her online after searching for tailors who could alter my mother's wedding gown. She was one of the few results that popped up, and after visiting three different shops, she was decidedly the clear winner. She assured me she could remove the yellow stains and the long sleeves and billowing train to transform it into a simple sleeveless dress with a slight drop in the back hem.

By the third visit, she had removed the sleeves and wanted me to try it on to ensure that the arm openings fit.

"Your skin is so pale," she said, observing that my white arms nearly matched the color of the dress.

I told her my story, and I could see tears filling her brown eyes. She told me about her sister who had cancer and the other friends she knew who'd had it. Cancer always seemed to be a unifying topic. We became fast and easy friends, and I learned to understand her Vietnamese accent.

I stared at myself in the shop mirror in disbelief, never thinking I would be wearing a white wedding dress with a big diamond on my left hand. As a young girl, I thought I wanted to get married when I was 25 to a handsome man and maybe have one or two kids. Twenty-five was my favorite number. I knew I didn't want a lot of children like we had in our family, but I thought it would be all right to have one or two.

By the time I was a teenager, kids were out of the equation. They were too much work, and I didn't want to be a mother or caregiver, period. And that night at the party when I was a teenager had left me deeply scarred and conflicted about men. In college, I still thought I'd eventually have a husband, but my 25th birthday was around the corner, and I wasn't ready to give up my independence. I loved being single and unattached, with no one to answer to, no one to worry about—but I still wanted a person. Girlfriends filled that void. As I became more and more involved in social-justice activities and found myself surrounded by staunch feminists and activists, I almost felt guilty for even wanting to be with a man. Some women spoke about men and their chauvinism and egos, their power plays, and obsession with sex. Hanging around all these seemingly powerful and content single women made it easier to go without. Plus, the unhappy married couples I knew gave singlehood another affirmative vote. I received lots of encouragement from my single friends, along with plenty of "I wish I could have the same freedom you have" from my married acquaintances.

It was the perfect solution to so many questions. It was easy not to have kids as a single woman. It was easy to avoid being taken advantage of by a man if I stayed single. I didn't want to need anyone. I could be a strong single woman on my own.

Yet, now I was standing before the three-way mirror with the late summer sun shining through the windows, happier than I'd ever been in my life, ready to say "I do" to a man I loved more than I thought possible. A man who loved me more than I could fully understand.

Who stayed at my bedside through all my treatments, watching every move the nurses made, and correcting the new ones who misstepped. Who proposed on our worst day despite the uncertain and possibly very short future. Who, for whatever reason, allowed me to guide him up mountains and choose routes that always led to precarious rock gullies or steep talus slopes. I couldn't find my way through a shopping mall and get back to my car, yet he let me lead him up trailless hillsides. My illness helped me see my strength in a new light. I could be strong *with* someone.

I found Alan when I finally allowed myself to be open to a relationship. I'd had an epiphany years before on a backpacking trip to Utah when I spent a night away from the group. I had thought I needed to prove I could be alone, but I realized that night being alone was like any other night I spent by myself. What I needed to learn was not how to survive by myself, but how to live with others and not lose myself in the process. That epiphany helped me find the hiking group and begin making closer friends. I also realized I wanted a deeper connection. The sterile life that I'd built for myself was becoming stuffy and stifling. I wanted others in my life who shared my interests, and I was ready to trust again. I had come a long way from my bottled-up angry years, and in learning to make peace with my past, I could finally open myself to a new future. I'd loved a man before, but my love for Alan was unlike anything that I'd felt for another person.

The morning of our wedding, we met with the priest who was officiating our ceremony. He also happened to be a very good friend of mine, but this was the first time that he'd met Alan. We told him about how we'd met and what we enjoyed doing as a couple. We sat laughing and talking, recalling the major events of our 2½ years of dating.

"How did you know you loved Alan?" my friend asked.

I smiled and looked at Alan, and then back at my friend. It was an easy answer. In the weeks and months after his mom broke her hip, Alan was taking care of her at her home in Laramie, 140 miles away. It was a difficult time for him, and us, and despite stress-filled words, emotion-induced standoffs, and days of silence, we stayed together. I realized I loved him then even if he didn't love me back. I knew that I had found a friend and companion, and experienced as true a love as I'd ever experienced, and I wanted to enjoy it for as long as my body would allow me to stay on this earth.

---

The irony that I'd found someone and almost immediately gotten sick seemed fitting, as if it could be another verse to my favorite song, Alanis Morissette's *Ironic*. My lyric would be, "it's like a death sentence when you just want to live. It's like finding a man, when you've given up on them."

It had been a frigid New Year's Eve. A friend was hosting a party and all my hiking buddies were going to be there. I really wanted to go, but I also really wanted to stay home curled up on the couch with my beagle. Despite the weather, I drove the 45 minutes up to the foothills. I almost turned back around as I entered the neighborhood due to all its snow and limited parking. I looked down at the container with a huge hunk of blue cheese, honey, and walnuts sitting in the passenger seat. It would go to waste if I didn't go to the party. Besides, I had made it all the way up the hill and through the cul-de-sac hell of suburbia, so I told myself to I was going to the party.

I knocked on the door, and one of my friends pulled it open and a smile ripped across her face.

"You made it! I'm so glad."

I instantly felt at home and was part of the crowd, as I set down my cheese and dropped off a bottle of wine at the table where several bottles were lined up like soldiers. How great to have a group of friends again. It had been years, probably since college, when I'd had more than just a couple friends to hang out with.

I knew most everyone, and we exchanged happy hugs and New Year's greetings, along with tales of our drives through the snowy streets and near-zero temperatures. I poured myself a glass of wine, and settled in at the small kitchen table with a couple of friends.

The door opened and yet another round of greetings began. I glanced over my shoulder and saw it was the same cute blonde guy that I'd met when our group of friends had gone to the movie theater a month ago. *Oh, he's here,* I thought, smiling as I remembered our evening at the theater when my friend Ed directed me to the only open seat, which was between Alan and another guy. I was happy I decided to drive up the hill, and made my way over to greet him.

"Hi Alan—it's good to see you."

He looked at me blankly. I could tell he was trying to remember my name. My heart sank.

"Rochelle. We met at the *127 Hours* movie." I hoped to jog his memory.

"Oh, right. I knew you looked familiar. How are you?"

We talked about the weather and the roads, and luckily other friends came over so I could take my bruised ego back to the kitchen. Passing the table full of wine, I wished I had a designated driver so I could pour myself an entire bottle.

"So, do you make resolutions?" my friend asked, as I sidled up to the table where she sat.

I smiled, wondering how she knew that this was the first year that I'd really made a true resolution, a resolution that meant something. The irony was that my resolution had just slapped me in the face. I thought about making something up, but I'd recently been reading about the power of putting your goals out into the universe, and decided, *what the hell*. I was just rejected by Alan; perhaps this would be a little revenge.

"My resolution is to be open," I confided, "to a relationship in particular."

My friend's eyebrow lifted, and she smiled slyly.

"Really?" she said, looking over at her partner, who also had the same grin on his face.

"I know. Crazy, right?" I laughed again. They'd found each other through our group of hiking friends, like many others who had coupled up.

"That should be an easy resolution," her partner said, as they rattled off the remaining single guys in our group of mutual friends, including Alan. I hoped they were right, although none of the guys had asked me out yet, so I wasn't feeling too confident about her prediction. And after the crushing realization that Alan hadn't even remembered me, I questioned my ability to attract anyone. After all, we had sat next to each other for over 2 hours. I touched his arm as we said goodbye after the movie, and I mentioned how nice it was to meet him. That was a huge flirty move on my part, but evidently not so much for him.

Alan eventually got the hint after that New Year's Eve party. We went on a snowshoe hike with our mutual friends in January, and he threw snow at me like a schoolboy teasing a girl on the playground—my first clue. On the next group hike, he offered to be the rear leader to make sure there were no stragglers left behind. I made a point to slow my pace and chatted him up on the walk down. I asked more about his home state of Wyoming, and we talked about sports and hiking. I wanted to sit by him at the restaurant after the hike, but only single seats remained when we arrived. A few days later he emailed me, asking if I'd want to go to an NBA basketball game. Growing up as a basketball fan, I eagerly agreed. He'd finally gotten the hint. From that first real date at the basketball arena, to hundreds of miles of hiking and mountains climbed together, we had made it to our wedding day. Me in a simple white wedding dress, about to say "I do" to the man who at first hadn't remembered me.

A year ago, I had been falling apart, blubbering like a baby, feeling like a failure as a cancer patient, inadequate as a woman, and a quitter. On our wedding day, I felt powerful, strong, and blissfully happy.

---

I hadn't been sure we'd get a real wedding; I had worried it would be a rushed affair with just a few witnesses. Or worse, that I'd be saying "I do" from a hospital bed. Never did I imagine that we would celebrate at an outdoor ceremony in the ponderosa pines, with the Rocky Mountains as a backdrop, a bright blue sky and crisp fall air, my favorite time of year. We stood before our family and friends, and easily professed our love to one another. It wasn't just a celebration of our marriage, but a celebration of life and of everything that those in attendance had done to support and get us to this place. My heart never felt more joy, peace, or love. They were the reason I was alive. Alan was the reason I wanted to live. Our life together is what I wanted to experience; what I didn't want to leave. I easily said goodbye to my single years and embraced my new role as a married woman. My heart was mended. I was healthy and blissfully in love. It was a melanoma miracle.

*nine*

———

# Getting Knocked Down

I laid down on the exam table as the doctor pressed his fingers along my neck, performing the usual check for any swollen nodes. It had been a year since the lucky Friday the 13th visit—and it had been a most wonderful year at that with our wedding being the highlight.

"The lung nodule lit up on the PET scan," he said as he pulled my arm up to check the lymph nodes in my armpit.

I felt every muscle in my body freeze—except my eyes. They burned with the sting of tears that had welled up, and I blinked furiously. I turned my head away from him, looking at the opposite wall, and trying to will the tears to go away. The doctor put his arm on my shoulder gently and I turned towards him. He looked me in the eye, "Do not give up. I am not giving up on you."

I looked at him and blinked away my tears. Our eyes locked, and I knew he'd get me through the ordeal. He had gotten me this far.

Right before the wedding, my PET scan showed a new nodule on my lungs. It didn't light up as cancerous; the doctor explained that some people develop these types of nodules, which are benign. Because it didn't light up on the scan, they concluded all was well and to just watch it to see if it changed.

The wedding excitement had distracted me from the results, but it didn't make sense, given my history. I didn't believe many stage four cancer patients got new noncancerous nodules. The 3 months between scans brought bouts of worry and anxiety attacks. I kept a watchful eye on my breathing—any shortness of breath sent shivers down my spine. I found myself scrutinizing every breath and every ache. I was biking to work, sure that my hard breathing was due to a tumor and not just the steep hill I had just climbed. I sat on the couch meditating and could feel my lungs closing in on me. I thought I was suffocating, and began picturing what it would be like to die of lung cancer—of not being able to breathe.

Yet, I convinced myself I was fine and just paranoid. It wasn't the first time I imagined diseases I never had. When the December scan arrived, I sat in the tube willing a clear picture, while sensing something was wrong. The same feeling that I had experienced going to that biopsy with the four white coats.

"What do we do now?" I asked.

My doctor always wanted to see the scans and view the images with his own two eyes. He never relied solely on the radiology report; instead, he insisted upon scrolling through the thousands of images to find that pink-lighted blob on his own. This time he didn't even trust his own eyes, and wanted his radiologist to also confirm the diagnosis. He escorted me and Alan down to the hospital's basement where the radiologists are privileged to sit in dark rooms and pore over gray-and-white images of flesh and bones intermingled with pink tumor spots.

They pulled up my scan and quickly located the culprit. The radiologist confirmed that it looked like a tumor.

"Can we biopsy it?" the doctor asked.

They discussed the options and ultimately both concurred that the tumor was situated in a terrible place to be biopsied. I would have to hold incredibly still and hold my breath for a lengthy period to avoid doing damage to the lung. I was quite confident that I would not be able to do either of those tasks; thankfully they decided to forgo the procedure. We assumed it was melanoma and attacked it appropriately, which meant a different kind of immunotherapy.

New treatment options had been announced in the 12 months since my original treatment. Thankfully, they didn't involve week-long hospital stays or 20 pounds of water-weight gain with every round. It was like normal cancer care—an infusion every 3 weeks. I shouldn't lose my hair, and the side effects didn't sound too bad—rash, itching, possibly diarrhea—and of course, a longer list of other more scary, possible, but not likely, symptoms.

All that was going through my mind was our honeymoon coming up in February, less than 2 months away. Alan and I never planned anything. We picked our mountains and outdoor adventures based on the weather, sometimes only landing on a location the night before. Twice we had planned trips—the first being Utah, and the second being our honeymoon trip to New Zealand. We knew what had happened in Utah—and now it appeared that melanoma would strike again. I began to wonder if I would ever plan anything.

My self-pitying thoughts grew larger, deeper, and darker. I blamed myself, thinking I had to be the cause of the recurrence, just as the original cancer had been my fault with my sun-obsessed baby-oil tanning and long days in a tube top detasseling Iowa corn fields. Not to mention the years of putting up with toxic people and never standing up for myself, a silent inner torment. I wrote angry words in my journal, berating myself for any positive thought or notion that implied I had any right to live. I was convinced that I deserved to die with my self-righteousness. F-bombs littered every sentence.

A few hours later, I realized I was going through the stages of death. I was surprised that I hadn't experienced this rage when death first knocked at my door. I must have stayed in the denial phase, with the lung tumor pushing me headfirst into anger and bargaining.

I was a mess. I couldn't stay positive, but still felt I could live. But I was also pretty sure that I would die. The tumble of emotions—the constant battering—reminded me of rafting white-water rapids. Bobbing up and down, bouncing off rocks, yelling and screaming, shouts of glee mixed with terrifying fear.

That image was so powerful, I decided to let myself ride the rapids in my mind to see where it would take me.

I tucked my body in tight and held on for dear life. The water flowed all around me, sometimes violently smacking me into the rocks. I continued to hold on, and let my body just go with the white foam. I rolled to the left and then the right, my body riding the waves wherever they went. Eventually the rocks and rapids eased, and I was floating on a gentle flowing river. I began to relax, and Jesus came to pick me up and put his arms under my body and carried me to the shore.

It was a crazy image for me. I've never "seen" the Catholic school Jesus before. I gave up on the man-like God images years ago. It was a little unnerving but comforting. I just had to ride this wave. Smooth waters are coming.

———

Needing more than mental reassurance, I sent an email to my friend John. We had been staying in touch as he received treatment for his recurrence. I'd been on my cancer-free cloud cheering him on from my "safe seats", but now I was back on the cancer field.

Our year and a half pen-pal friendship grew across the keys and cyberspace. Our emails were peppered with positive notes and humorous takes on cancer, and his realization that he *gets* to shovel snow. He shared the details of his scans and treatment options, using the medical jargon I refused to memorize. But his real gift was his ability to articulate the fear and anxiety of living with an unpredictable disease that made me feel less crazy, or at least not alone in my craziness.

We had never gotten together in person, although he had invited us to his gratitude party just months after we started corresponding, and I almost invited him to our wedding. Now after 18 months of email correspondence, I decided to ask if we could meet. I would be undergoing the same new treatment that he was finishing, and I was curious about what to expect. I also felt compelled to express my gratitude in a more personal way, to go beyond the typed words. I wanted to thank him for the hope he had given to me to arrive at this point on the survival curve, and subconsciously I feared it could be my last opportunity to meet my angel in person.

I brushed aside any worries of awkwardness, as I typed out my email informing John of my latest results and boldly asked if we might meet in person. He quickly responded with an invitation to come over for dinner. His wife, Janice, and Alan were both copied on the note. I wrote back, asking Janice what I could bring, and she asked me to bring a green salad.

Two weeks later, I stood in front of my closet, pushing hangers back and forth trying to figure out what to wear. *Should I dress up? Go casual?* I decided jeans and a sweater would be a happy medium. I was oddly nervous to meet John despite our year and a half of notes.

I held the salad bowl on my lap and followed the directions on my phone as we drove through the dark January cold. We pulled up to the house and parked by their mailbox. It was a nice ranch home in an established neighborhood. I inhaled deeply, opened the car door, and stepped out into the cold air. I carried the salad and nervously walked up their driveway to the front door, Alan following along with a bottle of wine in one hand. Before we could ring the bell, the door opened, and John filled the space with his 6-foot-plus frame as Janice stood at his side. He seemed even taller than I recalled when he stood up at the park.

"Welcome, come on in," he said, motioning us inside the narrow entryway.

I stepped up and our eyes met. I mumbled some sort of greeting and we introduced ourselves. I wanted to hug him, but the salad bowl made it awkward. We walked into the open area between the living room and kitchen.

"So, this is the new kitchen," I said, remembering John's note about their remodeling project and wanting to live long enough to enjoy it.

"Yes, it's been quite a project," Janice responded as she took the salad and set it on the counter.

They took turns telling the story about their home improvement adventures, describing their old kitchen and pointing out what used to be where. The conversation flowed easily as we swapped homeownership challenges.

"Janice likes to bust down walls," John quipped.

"It's how I cope," she stated.

And with that, the talk shifted to more serious matters. The reason we were even in their newly remodeled kitchen. The elephant now acknowledged, John and I stole the show as we reminisced about our weeks in the sub-intensive care unit, as we compared notes on how itchy we felt and how much weight we had gained. Janice and Alan piped in their observations as well, reminding us of details that we'd forgotten or were too drugged to even recall.

"How's the Yervoy?" he asked.

"I had one infusion on Tuesday, and I haven't noticed anything."

"It's a lot easier than IL-2," he laughed. "No, I haven't had many problems. Did they give you the Leukine?"

"They did. You didn't tell me it was a shot!" I chided.

A smile crept across his face. "I wasn't sure if I should tell you. I didn't know what you'd think about giving yourself a shot in the stomach. And I figured that you'd find out soon enough."

I leaned my head back and laughed. "It's probably good you didn't."

And so on we continued, each of us relating our tales of stage four melanoma from the first mole to the shocking days when we both found out it had spread. So many similarities, yet stark differences. Our main bond was the sense of helplessness juxtaposed against a fierce hope and belief in the new treatments.

We settled into our dining chairs and feasted on the most delicious beef stroganoff I had ever tasted. John poured the wine, and we toasted to new friends. We discovered more shared interests and backgrounds. John hailed from Minnesota, and Janice had relatives in Iowa. By the end of the evening, we felt like we'd known each other for much longer than 18 months, and that we'd certainly spent more time together than this one dinner. It was a delightful evening, and obvious that we were immediate friends.

As we stood in the same spot where John greeted us just hours earlier, I asked if I could give him a hug. He nodded and opened his arms.

"Thanks so much for having us," I said, as I wrapped my arms around his waist. He gave me a little squeeze, and I moved over to Janice and embraced her firmly.

"We'll have you over next time," I said as we walked out the door and down the driveway.

---

The doctors scheduled my new treatment to start in January. It was a four-dose regimen with 3 weeks between doses. I assumed our honeymoon would be delayed. We were scheduled to leave on February 21 and return on March 8—right in the middle of the four doses. The doctors both encouraged yet remained skeptical about the trip; believing we could do it, but also warning of potential side effects, describing what to do if something happened while we were backpacking in New Zealand. Luckily, the trip dates fell right in the 3-week window between the third and fourth treatments, and it didn't interfere with the dosage schedule. It was a question of whether I wanted to take the chance of being in New Zealand with any serious side effects. The doctors left it for me and my husband to decide.

It was an easy call, just like Utah. We would go. Besides, if my illness really was moving me closer to the end, I wanted to go to New Zealand before I felt worse.

The only minor glitch was the new drug, Leukine, that my oncologist recommended to go along with the infusions of Yervoy. Like the first visit when she explained the various treatment options, she optimistically described a recent study that showed that it boosted the infusion's effectiveness and didn't cause any additional side effects.

It seemed like an easy add-on with some potential benefits. The doctor sent me home with the research study, along with vials of the medicine and syringes. More belly shots. At least I'd become a pro at self-injecting.

Unfortunately, I made the mistake of reading the research summary and immediately became depressed. It was clear that the addition of the Leukine injections were only marginally more effective than just the use of Yervoy alone. Statistics still showed patients dying at high rates, and the study clearly stated that the drugs were shown to stabilize the disease's progression but not cure it. All this might do is give me a little more time.

My heart was heavy as I read those words. My shot at a cure was clearly gone. I hit the IL-2 home run, but someone in the stands threw the ball back while I was still standing at the plate. I looked out to center field; there were no bleachers, no option for a home run. The wall went up to the heavens. There was no home run in this ballpark. The best I could do was get a little more time on the field. Winning seemed out of the question.

On top of my life-threatening tumors, I also had a cold from hell as we prepared for our honeymoon. It was the kind that made my head feel like it is stuffed with a million cotton balls. My head was throbbing like a bass drum. My throat was sore and scratchy. I should not be in enclosed spaces with other human beings. But our trip was not work travel, and there simply was no canceling or delaying a honeymoon that we'd planned for 6 months. I was going on this trip. We had 48 hours before we met our tour group. Surely, I'd feel better in 2 days' time.

I sipped a brothy noodle concoction in the airport and swallowed cold medicine before we boarded our plane for the 14-hour flight to Auckland. Alan sat on the aisle, I sat in the middle, and a young woman sat next to me by the window. I tried not to cough or sneeze, or make any other obvious gestures revealing the germ fest in my body. I looked around for a flight attendant to ask if they could put my cooler containing my drugs in a refrigerator.

I bought the purple lunch cooler bag—on sale—to store my medication. It contained little bottles of Leukine powder and sterile water. I threw a keychain on top of them—one of those promotional tchotchkes with a thermometer and a compass—so I could monitor the cooler's temperature. The doctor warned me not to let it get warmer than 50 degrees Fahrenheit. A cheap bag and ice packs were fine for short flights, but I wasn't confident it would last 14 hours. I crossed my fingers, hoping I could convince a nice flight attendant to store the bag in the plane's refrigerator. No dice—it was against all sorts of flight rules.

I imagined the powder crystals losing all their potency and almost begged her to reconsider. She graciously offered to bring me a bag of ice. I hoped it would be enough. Halfway through the flight, I reached down under the seat to feel the mushy insulated canvas bag. It didn't feel cold enough. I wanted to check the keychain, but was afraid to let the cool air escape and push the temperature over the critical 50-degree threshold. The minute we landed in New Zealand I pulled the cooler onto my lap. Holding my breath, I unzipped the top and pulled out the thermometer: 47 degrees. I had put all my faith into that cheap device and believed it was, indeed, 47 degrees.

We arrived in Christchurch on a gray and drizzly morning. By afternoon, the clouds had cleared, so we walked to the botanic gardens. It was an expansive park, spanning multiple city blocks with different areas of plantings including a central rose garden. The serenity of the rock path lined by every color in the rainbow took my mind off my jet lag and desire to find a bed to take a nap.

We walked hand-in-hand, marveling at the glorious flowers—roses, birds of paradise, red hot pokers (my favorite flower name), and the elegant flamingo flower with its heart-shaped fuchsia petals. The bird of paradise took me back to Ecuador and memories of sandy beaches, the lush-green Andes, and the small but beautiful garden outside the hospital where I had volunteered.

My senses had returned to death mode, studying every detail of the rose petals and the pillow-like blossoms of hydrangeas and begonias, mentally imprinting the images onto my brain so I could carry them with me into the afterworld. It was quite freeing to just be and gaze at the delicate beauty in front of me, without worrying about the right angle, sunlight, or perfect petal. Alan took lots of pictures as I walked slowly along the winding paths. These were our last hours alone before meeting our tour group.

Despite being introverts who preferred off-the-beaten path treks with no other humans, we had opted for a guided tour for our honeymoon, happy to let someone else figure out trailheads and logistics, what to eat, and where to sleep. We were excited to meet new people and imagined making friends from other countries, and having people to visit in the future. But I hadn't been battling cancer when we bought the tickets. Making new friends seemed pointless, and small talk a total waste of time.

My head throbbed with thoughts of life and death, trying to soak up every single second of my time on Earth. I completely unplugged from my phone and email, leaving my life behind. I was determined to be normal. As normal as I could convince myself that I was, despite my pale skin, kinky curls, and white hair, along with the vials of medicine and syringes carefully packed in my purple cooler bag.

Thankfully I only suffered a minor rash from the new treatment, along with a sore and swollen abdomen from the injection needle pricks. My legs felt fine, and on our first hike Alan and I chose to get out in front and stay with the 20-something trip leader, a bubbly blonde with a wide smile and sweet disposition. The magic of the high peaks and lush meadows immediately soothed my spirit and transported me to the peaceful place only nature provided. With every step I felt more alive, and my lungs expanded like the views sprawling out before me. I was alive and on a trail in New Zealand.

Our guide made us stop even though Alan and I wanted to keep going. We wanted to beat the storms and reach the ridge with stupendous views. We settled for the high shelf overlooking the wide valley with glaciated peaks all around. I looked down on our travel companions, many huffing and puffing and slowly making their way up the steep track. I smiled inside, knowing I was still able to out-hike others. We stood and gazed around at the mountains and jagged rocks above us. I squeezed Alan's hand and leaned onto his shoulder.

"I love you. I love this. How blessed we are to be here."

He squeezed my hand, let go and put his arm around me, pulling me in close and kissing the top of my head. "I love you."

The rest of the group and its chatter disappeared as the world became just us and the mountains. The warm air and building clouds cloaked us in their protective shield. I breathed deeply and closed my eyes, my eyelids dropping, nodding to the gods in gratitude as I wrapped my arms tightly around Alan's waist.

This was exactly what I needed—a break from work. Ten days surrounded by nature's abundant life in what could arguably be the most beautiful country in the world. Healing power emanated from the peaks and valleys, rose from the rivers, shone through the stars, and whispered in the silent nights. *Thank you*, I murmured, as I opened my eyes and looked up to the sky.

---

"Rochelle, you have to see the stars," Alan said excitedly as he opened the door. "Get up."

I loved full moons and clear starry nights. I slipped on my sandals and tiptoed outside. The darkness enveloped me. It was darker than any place I had ever been. The sky was inky black with splashes of white. I felt like I was on a tiny boat in an ocean of black waves and diamond-studded white caps. The stars seemed close enough to touch, so big against the clear backdrop of midnight blue, the silhouettes of mountain ridges barely visible against the dark sky.

"Oh my gosh," I whispered, reaching for Alan's hand. His arm was hugged around my waist, as we stared up at the bright lights twinkling back on us. I wanted to take a picture—to somehow capture this image of the stars and their big balls of light. I looked all around me, a 360-degree kaleidoscope of sparkling lights swirling in the infinitely deep sky. I wanted to move our bed outside to sleep under this shimmering blanket.

We stood in silence, bathed by the starlight and holding each other tightly. There were no words to adequately describe the beauty before us, or the miracle that we were standing there behind a sheepherder wagon that had been converted to rustic sleeping accommodations, our honeymoon suite, on a New Zealand sheep ranch.

My bladder had enough stargazing though, and I looked around at the open field to find a private spot to pee.

"Just go right here," Alan said. "No one can see you."

He was right. It was pitch black, and the house was far enough up the hillside that no one would notice me squatting in the grass. Alan walked around to the front of the wagon, and I took a few steps out into the open. It was so nice not to worry about bears, snakes, or any large critters—New Zealand had none of them. Staring at the stars, I thought, *this must be the best country in the world and by far the best bathroom view ever. Mountains to gaze at, and no wild animals that might eat me in the middle of the night or mid-squat.* I stood up, snapping more mental pictures, whispering my gratitude, and eventually walked around the wagon and up into its comfy confines. I looked out the window one more time before taking off my glasses and going back to sleep.

The next morning, we walked up to the main ranch house for breakfast, hearing lots of excited chatter before we even opened the door. The rest of our group stayed at the main house. We were the only couple to get our own wagon. Our tour companions were comparing notes, wondering who had mice in their room. Had anyone seen the one climbing up the curtain? Evidently, they had not had nearly as peaceful a night as we had. I looked at Alan and smiled. And they had thought our wagon was primitive. We did not have mice. And I bet they weren't peeing outside under a canopy of white starlight.

I pulled our sweet guide aside and asked about my purple lunch cooler. Luckily, the mouse conversation kept everyone thoroughly distracted as I slipped out into the morning sun. I looked up at the gray mountain ridge, at the crystal blue sky that had showered us with its velvety sheen last night.

I sat on the edge of the bed and opened the cooler my guide had returned to me. I grabbed a syringe and set the little vial of powder next to me. I pulled out the bottle of sterile water and plunged the needle into its rubber top, extracting the liquid and transferring it to the glass vial of powder. Waiting for it to dissolve, I then lifted my shirt and tucked it under my chin. I extracted the mixture and readied the syringe. With my other hand, I pinched my belly and plunged the needle into the roll of flesh, the quick sting a stabbing reminder of how different my life felt. I wished that mice were my biggest problem that day.

I stuffed the needle into my biohazard bag, along with the alcohol swab, and gathered up the rest of my things. I carried my backpack up to the house and rejoined Alan in the kitchen to make peanut butter and jelly sandwiches to take along for our trail lunch.

My legs reminded me that we had done some steep walking the day before, but I couldn't wait to get out on the next path. The trail ran through a swampy forest of towering rimu trees and thick ferns, dots of sunshine penetrating the dense canopy. It was a nice rolling route, perfect for running. I was happy another person in our group agreed to run with me. As I ran, I looked around as much as possible, taking in the sights, sounds, and smells of the damp forest. The earth gave off a pungent odor of moist dirt and damp plants. Swampy and humid but cushiony underfoot, as if the ground were a sponge of dirt and moss. It seemed remarkable to find myself running in the rainforest on a cloudless day in New Zealand. Oh, how easy it was to forget the sting of the needle and the threat of growing tumors while gliding along the enchanted forest floor.

---

I sat by the window with Alan next to me, as the van swayed and tilted with each tight curve up the canyon. At what seemed to be the highest point, our guide pulled off into a wide parking lot and directed our eyes to a waterfall tumbling down the cliff in a straight, white line. Gray cliffs ringed the road in a half circle.

Like a waterfall crashing down a cliff, my thoughts hurtled back to the spring days in Zion, surrounded by similarly bent cliffs where death closed in around me. The natural cathedral had held my prayers and carried my spirit out of the darkness. I was now back at nature's altar riddled with more tumors, needing her healing spirit. Tears welled in my eyes as I felt the power of the water and the solid walls penetrate my worries and calm my soul, allowing me to live in the moment and see the holy and sacred gifts of life in the basic earthen elements.

Our days were filled with one beautiful scene after another. Hikes up to peaks overlooking vast valleys. Kayaking in Milford Sound with puppy-like seals bobbing alongside and sunning themselves on rocks. Biking through forests and fields and around turquoise blue lakes. Backpacking in the rain. Walking across a swaying suspension bridge over a raging river. My gratitude grew in tandem with my awe of the surrounding scenery and the adrenaline of our adventures. I didn't know how I would be able to return to my work-life back home, much less the chemotherapy room the day after our plane was scheduled to land.

Those competing realities fought inside my head, and sometimes I wanted to just blurt out, "I have stage four cancer. I may never see this again. That's why I look like a freak show and that's why I'm quiet." As if explaining myself would somehow make me feel better, or make me less self-conscious about my half-straight, half-curly, part-white, part-brown hair, my translucent skin, and long-sleeved shirts.

I worked hard to stay in the moment, but I couldn't stop looking at the brown spots on my hands, or the curly mess of hair on my head. I didn't want to look at myself, and I couldn't help but imagine that everyone was looking at me too and wondering, *What the hell?*

The more I tried to conceal it, the stronger the hold the melanoma seemed to have on me. I thought pretending to be "normal" would be helpful—to simply act and look like everyone else. But I couldn't. I wasn't normal. I couldn't wear shorts or tank tops like the other women. I couldn't even pull my hair back in a neat ponytail or push it behind my ears; the frizz, curls, and wispy white hairs were unruly and too short to control.

In each town, our travel companions pulled out their phones and immediately searched for service. They opened social media apps to post photos or scroll through images and updates to stay abreast of what was happening back home. At first I paid no attention, glad my phone was tucked deeply away into my bag.

In the middle of the trip, as we drove through lush-green mountains flowing like emerald rivers, nearly everyone around us had their heads down, staring at their screens. I wanted to yell at them, tell them to pay attention, to savor the moment. But who was I to judge? *Who was I to tell them how to live their lives. Me? The dying girl? Do I have a right to say something? Maybe even an obligation? To convey the lesson I was so painfully learning and reluctantly accepting? Should I dare try to teach them?*

Instead, I looked around as most were staring at their screens, some with big smiles on their faces. I looked back out the window to see everything before it was too late and had passed out of sight.

---

Every night I'd recap the day in my journal, recalling the beauty I'd seen that day. This sometimes pulled me off my pity pot, and at other times only served as my pot to piss and moan in. One night I dove headfirst into self-pity, and instead of focusing on the present with its incredible blessings, I let fear take over as I imagined the tumors growing and eventually suffocating me. I knew this was a possibility; I understood that the treatment could possibly do nothing like the research paper suggested, and the tumors would continue growing. I shuddered every time I imagined my lungs overcome with globs of disease and not being able to breathe. Drowning. Suffocating. Eyes open and aware, yet unable to do anything but gasp. Panic rose in my chest, and I breathed deeply as if to remind myself and test my lungs to see if they were still functioning. They seemed the same as usual. I inhaled and repeated in my head, *I don't want to die. Please. I don't want to die.*

These thoughts stayed with me the next day as we drove along the mountains shrouded by clouds. The humidity was so thick you could see it. The clouds clung to the peaks and spread their white blanket across the summits. Slowly the sun rose higher in the sky, finding a break in the clouds; the rays shone down like beams of light onto the green valley floor. I imagined myself rocketing through the opening and flying to the heavens, grabbing my cousin, and begging for life. My neck tightened and eyes burned with tears that eventually spilled down my cheeks. I couldn't fight them. I gripped Alan's hand. He looked down at me and I looked back, repeating my mantra, "I don't want to die."

He squeezed my hand tight and leaned into me, "You won't."

I held tight as our shoulders touched, wanting to believe him. Wanting to believe in myself. And hoping no one heard me.

Life and death appeared in every peak, valley, lake, river, Milford Sound, and the sea. We followed the shore of the Tasman Sea for miles, the horizon a blur as low-hanging clouds blended with the gray-blue water. We stopped to enjoy the seashore at a popular local spot. Our knowledgeable guide pointed out a large pile of white rocks ahead of us. He described a local custom to write messages on a white rock to those who have died, believing those messages are sent on to the dead through the vortex of the sea.

I squirmed in my seat, feeling exposed as if everyone else knew I had been thinking about death, wanting to reach up through the clouds to my dead cousin. Here, I could write her a note on a rock. Death had such a grip on me that day that not even the vortex of the sea could pull me out of my pitiful mood. I watched as others walked to the water and smiled when Alan took off running, tore off his shirt, and dove into the foamy waves. I loved his spirit and pure joy. I wanted to bottle it, chug it, get drunk on it. But mostly, I wanted to live and love that man for as long as I could.

I wrote my message in my head and stayed on the bus, hoping the vortex would carry my note even though not written in black and white on a rock, and stacked at the edge of the sea.

---

We awoke to clouds and rain on the last day of our trip. I was secretly happy because the weather might cancel our snorkeling date with the seals. I had never snorkeled before, and deep water terrified me. I wasn't a swimmer. I didn't pass basic swimming as a 5-year-old, and was downright petrified of drowning. But I had agreed to go because everyone else wanted to snorkel. I was overjoyed when our guide said the water was too murky to be poking our heads underwater looking for whatever lurked beneath its now gray waves. I happily put on my hiking pants and stuffed my swimsuit deep into the bag.

The limestone path soaked up the moisture as we circled the peninsula walking up and down the gentle hills passing chalky cliffs, and listening to the waves crash against the shore below. I was happy to feel the salty breeze in my frizzy hair, but also felt melancholy about our last day in paradise. I didn't want to leave, wishing I could stay in this country of natural wonders. There was so much more to see. I could have stayed in each town for a week, a month, forever, each spot so beautiful and remote.

The clouds broke and the sun poked through the billowing white sky as we came to the end of the trail. Our last walk in the southern hemisphere. We got back on the bus; everyone seemed a little more somber as we headed toward the city. Maybe they were all dreading a return to real life. I knew I was.

I sat in my window seat in my usual silence, hyper-aware of every passing tree or field of domestic deer. The anxiety of life rose like the waves, and I kept telling myself to look outside. Pay attention to what you see because you'll never see it again.

The bus guide started talking on his little public announcement system. I definitely was going to miss his stories and sense of humor. He explained some geological phenomena that created a distinct erosion, which only occurred here in this location. The bus pulled off the road, and outside my window was a wall of clay-colored stone with ribs of flowing rock spread out from the top layer of dirt and grasses. The pillars of limestone had been worn away by water and wind, leaving fantastical shapes and what looked like melting candles.

I looked at Alan in surprise, and said, "It's like Bryce Canyon."

We stared at each other in disbelief. Our favorite and most magical place was again before us, the mystical shapes bringing smiles and wonder, and most of all, hope.

"I think that's a good sign," I commented, squeezing his hand.

He gave me a big kiss on the mouth, and I pressed my lips tightly to his.

"I love you."

"I love you too."

The magic of New Zealand worked. Three months after our honeymoon, I had another scan to see if the lung tumor had grown. It had disappeared. Another complete response.

"We don't often see this with this treatment," my doctor said.

"I don't like to do anything half-assed," I retorted.

He laughed and nodded his head.

Another bullet dodged. Melanoma 0, Rochelle 3. *Can we call it a game already?*

———

I wanted nothing more than to enjoy my new life as a wife, as the full and official boss at my workplace, and with a healthy body. Life could return to normal with a routine and normal pressures. No more diagnoses or treatment regimens. I wanted to be just a happy working girl who was finally in charge.

It felt so good to make decisions and not have to worry about what my boss thought. My vision of how to run our program was now a reality—not a secret wish or subtle countercurrent to the backbiting culture. I hoped that my team felt as free as I did.

That first year and a half after I had taken over flew by with easy victories and newfound partnerships. Of course, there were also some bumps and criticisms, but mostly my approach was met with open arms. In addition, the bigger paycheck took away any financial concerns. I bought a few new outfits and a new suit. One simple purchase in an airport sealed my identity as a successful and financially secure woman.

I had flown out on a Sunday afternoon for a Monday meeting in D.C. As I waited in the airport security line, I went through my mental checklist to ensure that I hadn't forgotten anything. Suit, check. Dress boots, yes. Socks and pajamas, in the side pocket. I put my hand up to my ears and felt the smooth metal of simple silver hoops, and looked down at my wrist for my two-toned dress watch. Then I felt my neck for the tiny diamond pendant, but there was just bare skin. And I planned to wear two V-neck sweaters under my suit jacket.

I beat myself up for the oversight. I'd packed for so many business trips that I did it by rote. I always wore the same earrings and necklace, which made packing so much easier.

Walking towards my gate, I decided to duck into a gift shop to see if I could find a suitable replacement. Most necklaces were a bit gaudy or too western for my taste with big turquoise pendants and lots of dream-catcher designs. I walked over to the other carousel of jewelry and noticed a small silver pendant with flecks of burgundy and deep violet. My suit for this trip just happened to be dark gray, and my shirts were either purple or mauve. The necklace matched perfectly.

I held the necklace, trying to rationalize impulse buying jewelry in an airport for two days of meetings. A little voice reminded me that I was not that penny-pinching entry level worker struggling to pay the bills. I was a boss with a nice salary. I could afford it, and not worry that it would cut into my grocery money.

I looked down at my brand-name jeans, expensive running shoes, and fancy logo on my luggage and smiled.

Clutching the pendant, I strode over to the counter, pulled out my wallet, and handed the cashier the blue credit card that I'd had since college.

My first frivolous purchase. OK, maybe not the first frivolity, but certainly the first purchase that wasn't planned, fully researched, or on sale. That felt good.

*ten*

—

# Hearing Voices

I t had been about 18 months since I'd received the all-clear result from the lung tumor. My job, once again, had started stressing me out. Despite being the boss and finally having the authority to make decisions and create my vision for our department, the frequent work travel, meetings, and big presentations simply had worn me out. I had started getting headaches again, and I treated what I wryly called "rot gut" with antacids that had become a daily part of my diet. A business trip to Portland seemed the perfect time to add a little side trip to the coast. My natural antidote.

Alan met me after the meetings, and we drove to the southern coast of Oregon and slowly made our way north up the Oregon Coast Highway 101. The ocean did not disappoint with her wild white waves and rugged coastline. We pulled into the parking lot of a beach-side park, and I distinctly remembered a sign warning of sneaker waves. "A sneaker wave can strike without warning . . . with enough force to knock you down and drag you into the ocean. Don't turn your back on the ocean."

After the first cancer recurrence, I had written a poem about the waves of the "C"—C being cancer, of course. That warning sign on the beach spoke to me, as I worried about my maladies and stomach churning. I knew the C could come back at any time, just as it had with the sudden lumps and internal tumors. I tried not to turn my back, but often I wanted to just forget about the damned sneaker waves and leave the "C" alone.

However, the waves kept coming, and the mysterious sneakers along with the calm seas.

My oncologist encouraged, in fact demanded, that I schedule a mammogram. I protested. "Really? I get whole body PET scans every 3 months. Those detect cancer anywhere. Do I really need a mammogram?"

"Yes, you still need a mammogram. They can pick up much smaller tumors. By the time it would show up on a PET, it could be quite large."

I swallowed hard, and remembered the little lumps on my back and ribs that had been too small to show up on a scan.

I dutifully went in for my first boob-smashing. I am not well endowed, so to get my little girls into the machine felt like I was being pressed so hard against the apparatus that I might just become permanently affixed.

The tech told me to hold still as she lowered the contraption and squeezed so tight I thought my flesh would squirt right out of my nipples. She checked the monitor, told me she didn't have a good read, and would need to do it again. *Oh joy*, I thought. This was like the phlebotomists who could no longer find a vein and had to go fishing. Even my boobs weren't reliable. *Why can't I be a one-and-done kind of patient? I always used to be.*

Until I became a patient with a foot-thick medical record and ruined veins—and always an A cup.

After finally getting a good image, she told me that I'd get a call with any results if they're out of the normal range, or just a letter if it's normal.

"I'll wait for the letter," I told her and walked out.

I wasn't worried about the mammogram. I had other irons in the fire: a big work project and my mother-in-law wasn't doing well. I needed to pick up a few things and take them to the assisted living facility where she lived, but first I went home to feed Junior. He ran around excitedly, anxiously waiting to be let out into the backyard. I dropped my things and filled up his food dish before letting him back in. I was getting ready to walk out the door and my phone rang. It was the doctor's office.

I hit the button, "Hello."

A sweet voice responded, "I'm calling from radiology about your mammogram results. It showed some abnormalities. You will need another mammogram and an ultrasound. When can we schedule those for you?"

I held onto the counter as the caller's words knocked the wind out of me like a sucker punch to the gut. Abnormalities? Another mammogram? And an ultrasound?

I looked around frantically for my work phone with my calendar. Junior followed, pawing at my leg, as I fumbled with the two phones and a note pad. The receptionist offered a few appointment openings; the only one that worked was the same time as my staff meeting. I didn't care. I would cancel it. Or just quit. Walk away before they buried me.

I hung up the phone, and my legs buckled. I lost the strength to stand and fell to my knees, my hands gripping the wood floor as my body shook with sobs. I gasped for air, my mouth open, breathing hard. Tears rained down from my eyes as I laid on my side, resting my head on the floor. I pulled up my knees, clutching them tightly as I curled into the fetal position. Spit dripped down the side of my mouth, mixing with the tears that rolled down my cheeks, forming a pool of salty drool. My tears were uncontrollable. My anger so palpable. I couldn't believe this was happening. My mind spun out of control, picturing new treatments, losing my hair, throwing up, feeling like crap. *Oh shit— I didn't want* that *kind of cancer.*

My dog leaned into my face as I rocked myself back and forth. I wrapped my arms around him and pulled him in close, grateful to have his warm heart beating next to me. I stroked his fur, wishing I could make this all go away as I let myself cry.

I knew Alan would be waiting for me, so I kissed Junior on the top of the nose and wiped my eyes as I pulled myself off the floor. I sent a quick text to let him know I was finally on my way. I gave another kiss to my fur baby and went out to the car.

As soon as I shut my car door, anger erupted like a volcano. I screamed—a bloody murder scream that I had never heard before, one that came from the depths of my gut, but felt like it was coming from someone else. I screamed every cuss word I knew as I pleaded with the gods or whoever would listen. *I can't have cancer again. Please. I can't.*

I sat in the waiting room, hoping the doctor would come tell me the second mammogram was fine, and that there was no need for an ultrasound. Another woman, about my age, sat across from me. I wasn't paying much attention to her until a tech came out and spoke to her. I recognized her fear—the blank stare as the blood drained from her cheeks. My heart broke for her. I felt her pain. I wanted to do something. To walk over to her, and hold her. Say something. I tried to meet her eyes, but she only stared straight ahead, and then down at her phone.

I closed my eyes until I heard my name called. I looked up at the technician, and the familiar hot rush of fear coursed through my veins so fast I thought I would faint. It was supposed to be the doctor. A tech meant more images. I forgot about the other woman as I entered my own world. I said nothing as the tech led me back into the exam room and asked me to lie down on the table.

I stared at the pink and beige curtain that hung by the door as she squirted the warm goo on my breast. I focused on the curtain, studying its paisley pattern, trying not to think of anything. The tech moved the wand over and around my breast, and I saw out of the corner of my eye the screen with the ultrasound images. I turned my head to look at the monitor. All I saw were black and white blobs. I didn't know if the blobs were normal. What did a tumor look like on an ultrasound? Did it turn pink like the tumors on a PET scan? I studied the screen and its moving blobs, trying to see whether anything pointed obviously to cancer. What about that weird-shaped blob at the top? Or that red spot? What was that? The tech said nothing as she kept cruising the wand around the top of my breast like a matchbox car making laps on a track. She finally paused and hit a button on the screen.

"I don't see anything, but I'll check with the doctor and be back," Her voice was calm as she wiped off the goo and put the wand back in its holding device.

I closed my eyes as emotions rose from my chest. I clenched my jaw, my fingernails digging into my palms as I fought back tears.

"You OK?" The tech asked.

Not daring open my eyes for fear of the flood they contained, I nodded and barely whispered, "Yes."

I'm sure she thinks I'm crazy. She told me she hadn't seen anything, and I'm turning into a blubbery mess. I should be relieved, happy even, and there I was fighting a geyser of tears.

She walked back into the room and said the doctor concurred. There was nothing to worry about. I could put my clothes back on and go home.

I still couldn't speak. I tried to smile and nod as she reminded me how to get back to the little locker where I stored my clothes. I slid to the end of the exam table;

my body feeling like rubber as I put my feet on the floor. I held onto the table and pushed myself up, hoping my legs wouldn't buckle. I slowly shuffled out through the wide door and down the hallway, trying to recall whether she said left or right turn at the end of the hall. My mind raced as my heart still pounded in my chest. *I was going to be fine,* I kept telling myself. But I didn't quite believe it. Something was certainly *not* fine.

My work world was filled with brainy researchers and intellectual policy experts. It was all very heady. Personal topics barely made it to even the cocktail hour receptions. There might be a mention of kids or a spouse, but very little real-life discussions occurred.

I had thrived on the separation between work and my personal life, never one to hang out at the proverbial water cooler or swap gossip in the halls. Work was work. Life was life, and it was outside the brick building I occupied during the week. However, my inner sensitive self would gravitate toward any mentions of real-life challenges. It seemed that my sensitive voice started cropping up more often, wanting to be suddenly heard. She was in full force after my diagnosis, when I sent funny but vulnerable notes to friends and family. I looked for ways to keep her around, but too easily slid back into intellectual mode, leaving her heart behind as I climbed the company ladder and strode around in my business suits and jackets.

A few weeks after my mammogram, I was listening to a politician in the front of the room describe her achievements and future goals. She wore a nice suit and carried herself with a perfect balance of poise, professionalism, and approachability. I always sensed she was genuine, not just following a script or talking points. As she wrapped up her speech, she revealed that she was facing a personal challenge that might impact her work. She had a brain tumor.

My heart sank as I felt the weight of her words, and the memories of my own diagnosis weighing down on my shoulders and squeezing my chest. I wanted to hug her and hear more of her story, but sensed the discomfort from my colleagues as they shifted in their seats.

"But I will be at the Summit, and I promise to work hard for you," she said, quickly dismissing and covering up the collective anxiety with that favorite four-letter word—"work."

I glanced down at my notebook, and felt an urge to walk out the door and go home. People stood up and made their way to the door. A colleague stopped me and asked about an upcoming meeting. It took me a split second to switch back into work mode and remember what he was talking about.

"Oh, right. Yes, we're on for two o'clock. I'll have the latest numbers for you."

I looked over my shoulder to see the speaker standing by the podium, talking with another colleague. She didn't know me, and I dismissed any urge to walk over and introduce myself or otherwise acknowledge what she shared and to express my empathy. It was time to get back to work. I turned towards the door and joined the line of people making their way to the stairwells and elevators, trying to tune out the jumble of voices around me.

Six months later, I saw her at an event. She had successfully undergone surgery for her brain tumor and beamed with survivor's radiance as her husband stood next to her in his own glow. They were greeting a long line of attendees who wanted to shake her hand and introduce themselves.

Alan happened to be with me, and I whispered to him that she was the one with the brain tumor. He squeezed my hand and nodded.

My heart fluttered as I rehearsed our possible introductions. Most people just shook her hand and told her where they were from or for whom they worked. I stuck out my hand and, as she placed her silky fingers in mine, I wrapped my other hand around hers and looked her in the eye. I introduced myself and my position within the organization, and then introduced Alan as my husband.

"I'm so happy you are doing well. You look great. I'm a cancer survivor too. I wish you the best."

She looked back at me with her dark eyes and smiled. "Thank you," she said. "Thank you so much."

Her husband leaned in, "Thank you for sharing that. That means so much to us."

As we walked away, I grabbed Alan's hand, and he squeezed mine tightly.

"I had to say something," I explained.

I felt a smile on my face and a peace I didn't often feel at those schmoozy business receptions. That feeling quickly dissipated, however, as a lobbyist started rambling on about some policy he was working hard to change, telling us all the details about it. A server walked by with a tray of full wine glasses. I grabbed one and immediately took a big gulp.

The honeymoon phase of my promotion and leadership role was wearing quite thin. I enjoyed my job, and still felt a rush of adrenaline traveling to different conferences and meetings. Speaking in front of groups became second nature to me, and my networking skills advanced at the cocktail receptions. Yet, I increasingly found myself frustrated with the diligent and constant politicking. I'd moved back into the superficial zone of intellect, while still wanting to hold onto the person I found after I got sick. The person who sought out the legislator fighting cancer. The person who learned to live and be in the messiness of life.

Our dinners with John and Janice filled my need for true connection. We continued meeting on a somewhat regular schedule and took turns hosting. John had been battling more tumors, and a year and a half after our first dinner meeting, finally received some good news. They'd been traveling, and had just returned from an epic road trip. We sat outside on our deck and listened as they regaled us with the joys of road trips and spending lots of hours in a car with your spouse. He shared his latest scan results, and stated that things were looking better. Instead of just sharing one bottle of wine, we polished off a second. The joy and relief in their voices was so palpable after so many months with little improvement. Their happiness and their struggle another reminder of just how precarious life was and how quickly it could change.

They stayed late into the evening. None of us wanted this happy moment to end. We all knew the other side of this situation, and we held on tightly before it slipped away like the moon falling in the western sky.

---

Nearly 2 years had passed since the scan showing that the cancer spread to my lungs. I was feeling great and due for my next regularly scheduled PET scan. I didn't know how many I'd had; I'd lost track, but it was in the double digits. I wasn't worried. It was December, and I was ready for the holiday break. I felt good, had plenty of work obligations, and was confident that everything was fine.

I wore my standard PET scan metal-free uniform—blue-, pink-, and white-striped sports bra, navy-blue sweatpants, a burgundy t-shirt, and a long-sleeved shirt from my first marathon. The marathon shirt was my good luck charm, (or so I convinced myself to believe). I had worn it for every scan since the first one. And they'd all been good—except that pesky lung tumor. I ignored that slight aberration. It has been good luck more than it has been bad. The shirt was too big and starting to fray, but I didn't care.

I sat in the room waiting for the radioactive injection of glucose to circulate through my system. I pulled out my laptop and concentrated on the policy brief I needed to review and edit. Time passed quickly, and I was soon summoned to the scanning room. I situated myself in my usual position on the long table, snuggled into the familiar cocoon, and closed my eyes as the table rose and slid into the cylindrical machine. I made a mental list of agenda items for my staff meeting and emails I needed to send. I listened to the gentle whirring of the scanner, and told it there was nothing to see. I was clean. No tumors. I felt great.

At 4:30 that afternoon my office phone rang, the caller ID displaying my medical provider's name. I picked up the phone and heard the familiar accent of my oncologist. Turning my chair away, I pulled myself closer to the phone. The doctor never called me with results, only the nurse. A wave of nausea washed over me.

"The scan showed something on your ovary," she explained.

The wave crashed and I could barely hear what she said, the sounds were muffled as if I were deep on the sea floor. Something about an ultrasound, a gynecological oncologist, and tumor markers. I wrote down, "ovary, blood tests, tumor marker, CA-125, gyn-onc" on the list of to-dos that sat beside my computer. I stared out the window at the darkening sky as night descended on the parking lot below me.

The doctor paused. I could barely breathe. Her words had sucked the air out of my lungs and drained the blood from my face. My muscles turned into rubber, and I slumped in my chair.

"Are you OK?" she asked.

Pause.

"I think so." I said the words, not knowing if they were true.

I looked down at the words on the paper, and couldn't remember what to do. *What does CA-125 mean?*

*Tumor marker? Gyn-onc?* I asked the doctor to tell me again what I was supposed to do. She repeated the instructions. I scribbled more words on my paper and hung up the phone.

I leaned back in my chair and stared out at the dark sky. I closed my eyes. Devastated. Shocked. Stunned. Angry. This was the only PET scan I had gone into feeling confident that I'd come out with clear results. My melanoma reality washed over me like a tidal wave. I began smelling the hospital room where I spent weeks struggling through IL-2. I saw all the tumors on my first scan. I felt lumps all over my back. I heard the nurses talking to chemo patients as I watched the Yervoy drip down the IV tube into my arm. I couldn't believe it was in my ovary, another organ that when cancer strikes it kills. It had been in my lung. Now, it was in my ovary. I was mad. Sad, and scared.

I didn't want to tell Alan. Maybe I could come clean to him about it once all the tests are done and everything comes back as clear. *I can't tell him now. He's gone through enough.*

But I can't *not* tell him. I can't keep this pain to myself. *I'm sorry, Alan.*

I looked at the clock on my phone; it was 4:58 p.m. I grabbed my bag and walked downstairs and out into the cool dark night. I felt a sense of panic and urgency to schedule the ultrasound. 5:03 p.m. Maybe I could still catch someone. I pulled my phone out of my coat pocket and brought up the radiology phone number I had saved in my list of contacts and pushed the call button. I walked across the parking lot, listening to the phone ringing on the other end. Finally, after five rings a pleasant voice answered, "Radiology, how can I help you?"

"Uh . . . hello. Yes, I need to schedule a vaginal ultrasound. My doctor just placed the order."

She asked for my medical record number, and I rattled off the nine-digit number that had become as familiar to me as my phone number. She went over what to expect and what time to arrive. The appointment was for Wednesday morning, a mere 39 hours from now.

I looked around to see if anyone could have overheard my conversation, but saw no one. I took a deep breath and opened my car door, sinking into the seat's beige fabric, and leaning my head against the steering wheel as tears rolled down my cheeks. *When will I stop crying in my car?*

On Wednesday morning, I walked into the medical offices feeling depressed and angry. As it had with the mammogram, I sensed my body was sending "sneaker waves" like those that the beach sign had warned about, to remind me that life can change in an instant. I worried that my luck was running out. I had thoughts of leaving my job, but always pushed them away. The sneaker waves brought them back, however, making me question why I hadn't resigned. My old boss wasn't the only difficult person there, and I was getting fed up with the continued demands to ignore and work around those problem people. Now I was going to die, and I would still haven't listened to my gut feeling that's been telling me to walk away from a work culture that didn't fit my values. I was playing with fire, and I kept getting burned. When would I learn?

I glanced around at the faces in the waiting room, and felt just as sick as many of them probably were.

I'd gotten used to walking into this building with my head high, saying "thank you" to the universe as I walked confidently, healthily to my oncologist's office. Knowing I didn't belong or need to be here. Today, I felt like I belonged to the tribe.

After the internal vaginal probing, I walked across the waiting area to the lab to get my blood drawn. The nurse asked the usual name and date of birth questions and confirmed the blood-test order. I turned away when she said CA-125 tumor marker, "tumor" echoing in my ears.

Thankfully, she quickly found a vein with the first stick and filled the vial. She pressed the cotton ball onto my arm and wrapped it with medical tape. I wished her a nice day and left the office with my head held low, eyes diverting any contact from others. The tears were near bursting, as I looked down at the white-and-gray floor tiles and followed them to the exit for the parking lot. Once inside the security of my car, I leaned my head against the steering wheel and fumbled to put the key in the ignition. Again, I let a few tears roll down my cheeks and onto the steering column. I picked up my head, looked at my puffy red eyes in the mirror, and slowly backed out into the parking lot. I wanted to drive somewhere, anywhere, but my office. I told myself, *Everything would be fine. Pull it together. Go to work. You have a lot to do. It will distract you.*

I drove the long way back to my office, choosing to meander along the parkway lined with trees. It was as close to nature as I could get.

I couldn't concentrate at work, however, and broke all my rules of no internet research. I plugged in "melanoma spread to ovaries" into Google, to see what it had to say. I didn't think that ovaries were common destinations for melanoma. The brain, yes. Lungs, check. Liver, been there, done that. But not ovaries.

From the few articles I read, it didn't sound like a common occurrence. I chose to believe Google's truth and closed the browser.

The doctor had explained one possibility for the scan's result. Ovulation can sometimes cause the ovary to mimic a tumor; the chemical changes that take place in ovulation can cause the ovary to react to the radioactive sugar in the same way a tumor grabs the glucose and lights up.

I smiled. It made sense. It was that time of my cycle. Surely, that must be it.

But the ultrasound that was taken a few days after showed a distinct mass on my ovary. The mass was on my left ovary, but the PET scan had showed a tumor on the right ovary. The gynecologist read the radiology report over and over and called the radiologist to make sure there wasn't an error. No error. Another ultrasound would be needed to look again at the mass and determine its pathology. *Ugh.* I am admittedly a bit of a prude and having that ultrasound wand stuck up inside me was just not the most enjoyable experience. I empathized with the women with ovarian and cervical cancers. How invasive all those tests and procedures must feel. I hoped I was not joining their tribe.

The second ultrasound still showed the mass, and it was getting bigger, growing like the acid ball in my stomach. The gynecological oncologist assured me that it was benign because it didn't appear on the PET scan. It was large enough that it would have appeared as a pink spot on the scan. She conferred with my melanoma specialist and regular oncologist, and they all agreed that the tumor that lit up on my right ovary must have been due to ovulation, the mass on my left was a benign fibroid and it would hopefully dissolve on its own.

Ovulation. I told my doctors they could just take my ovaries. I had no intention of using them anyway.

It was two weeks before Christmas; my latest trip to cancer hell was over. I could breathe again.

---

Still reeling from the ovary fiasco, I tried to pull myself together and get excited about an upcoming work trip. I had been invited to join a group of policymakers on a trip to Israel at the end of the year. I left the day after Christmas.

Jerusalem. Jesus. The stations of the cross. Galilee. Lazarus. All these places and names I had heard in religion classes at school and every Sunday in church. And I was here, where Jesus walked and where he was crucified. Riding in a posh charter bus equipped with Wi-Fi along with policymakers from across the United States. It felt surreal to be in a place that had previously only existed as stories in my mind.

I didn't know whether I still believed in the historical version of Jesus and Catholic school theology that I had learned during my 16 years of religious education. Treading the same ground in the same city where so many were certain that Jesus had walked and performed miracles only raised even more questions in my mind. None of what I saw with my eyes matched the vision that I'd carried in my head of desert landscapes and sandy hills. This was a bustling city, its hillsides dotted with houses. There were cramped plazas around the Church of the Holy Sepulcher, and a Muslim Quarter with its own history and beliefs. Jerusalem felt tight and narrow, claustrophobic, and contradictory with its separate sections.

I grew up believing that this was the Holy Land, *our* holy land. After the Vatican, it was one of the holiest of places for a Catholic. Intellectually, I knew this was claimed as sacred space by others, but until I was immersed in and surrounded by the clashing cultures with their competing claims to its sovereignty and spiritual meaning, I had never understood the power of place. Yet, I belonged to none of them. I didn't identify with any of them.

I walked the streets as if I were holding the hand of my younger self, the little girl who believed the parable of the fishes and loaves, who had always felt sad during Holy Week when the church was stripped of its color, when the priests marched a big wooden cross down the center aisle. That younger self looked around wide-eyed, taking it all in, reconciling reality with her imagination while the adult me walked in doubt, wondering whether this really was the place that the Bible said it was.

I imagined my parents with their unflinching faith following me into these holy places. I wondered what they would do if they were here and saw the stone slab where Jesus was supposedly laid out after he died. Would they weep and bow their heads as I had observed an older woman do, kneeling before it? And what would they think of their daughter, a non-churchgoer—possibly even a non-believer—having the opportunity to touch that rock and look into the church and walk the streets where their Savior lived?

I felt guilty for my lack of faith and for questioning the historical veracity of the Bible stories, not trusting that the events it described had really happened but had been made up by humans to draw other believers to their altar. How could so many different religions claim the same space? Does that point to the universality of a spiritual homeland, or a human need for power and land? I tried to shake off my thoughts and questions, and allow the place to be what it was. I wasn't there on a spiritual quest.

I also wasn't sure why I had been chosen to accompany the work group to Israel. I didn't work in that area of our company. I cynically reasoned that it may have been because I had no children, and the trip took place over the Christmas holiday and New Year break. I had agreed to go because that Catholic schoolgirl remained curious about the Holy Land, and the policy wonk wanted to better understand the Jewish and Palestinian relationship.

A few days into the trip, our work group was hosted by a local family in Jerusalem for a Shabbat dinner at their home. We rode the bus in the dark through narrow streets, and were dropped off a block or two from their house. It looked like any neighborhood in any big city. The streets were full of cars, buildings were just feet from one another, and lights twinkled in the windows. We walked up the steps to the front door, and were greeted by a friendly young couple who warmly welcomed us.

Our group filed in, quickly filling the small kitchen and living room. The couple's children were all standing by the couch, smiling. After a frenzy of introductions, everyone settled around the long table. I sat towards the end, allowing others to sit closer to the hosts.

They described the rules for observing Shabbat. There were many questions about how they had prepared such an elaborate meal because electricity use wasn't allowed after sundown. They explained the prayer ritual and the children's roles. I watched as the children articulately answered questions and confidently took their places, showing reverence and respect to their guests and to the solemnity of the occasion.

The meal was like watching a replay of dinners at our Iowa farmhouse, like the evenings when my parents hosted engaged couples and served as their mentors for their Catholic wedding preparation classes. My siblings and I had been the same obedient and faithful youngsters following our parents' example, knowing our place and roles at the table and when we needed to go to our room and leave the adults to their conversations. My inner child couldn't help but join me at the table with her memories, and instantly bonded with the Jewish children across from her. Similar feelings of connection and community, with the spirituality I had experienced as a child, unfolded here in this simple apartment.

After the formal prayers, the hosts explained a family routine they used at dinner to promote conversation and sharing. Everyone had to answer the same question.

The question that evening was, "What is your life motto? And why?"

The lyrics of one of my favorite Tim McGraw tunes began playing in my head about living like you are dying. The chorus played repeatedly in my mind.

But I couldn't say that, because then I'd have to explain why. To admit that I was living like I was dying. Every scan, every mammogram, and ovary had been a reminder of it. What was I going to say? Maybe I could make something else up, like "Eat as much ice cream as possible." Something funny, or just simple. Maybe my old motto, "Live simply so that others may simply live." I half-listened to the answers given by others. Some were serious, while others were funny. But I spent most of the time dreading my turn and trying to come up with something other than the country tune. But my childhood memories and the familiar feeling of a spiritual community somehow pulled me out of my professional mode, and when my turn came, I blurted out, "Live like you are dying."

Lots of nods and smiles as if to say, *Good one, Rochelle.* I hoped they would just move on to the next person, but the host reminded me of the follow-up question.

"So, why is that your motto?"

His sweet face, his beautiful wife, their adorable children, all drew me into their world of holiness, sacred space, and ritual. I looked at him and calmly explained, "About four years ago, I was given about 9 months to live. But I'm still here. Maybe that motto sounds like a clichéd expression, but for me it is real. It has made me grateful for every day, and I try to remember it every single day."

The state senator next to me put her hand on my shoulder. Others looked at me in disbelief. I heard a few whispers, while a few looked at me, their eyes asking for more details, wondering how they did not know.

I looked down at my place setting and wished I could slide under the chair and somehow disappear into the black night.

Everyone stood to fill their plates with the food arrayed on the counter, while I made a beeline for the bathroom. I wanted to lock myself inside. I stood before the mirror, admonishing the woman looking back at me for being so open with people I barely knew and people who only knew my work self.

I took a few breaths, resumed my professional Rochelle persona, and walked out into the chatter and buzz of people filling plates and talking about food and politics. I took the last spot in line, and one of the women came over to me and whispered in my ear, "Thank you for sharing. You're an inspiration."

I relaxed a little, and scooped some vegetables onto my plate. I said nothing the rest of the night.

Two days later, we walked through the Garden of Gethsemane, the place where Jesus went to pray before his arrest. I was lost in thought, remembering the Bible story and imagining Jesus here in this very place before he was killed. Knowing, as the story goes in the book of Matthew, that he is going to die and asking that this cup pass from him, while realizing he must go forth. His path had been predetermined. I walked slowly, looking closely at the olive trees and shrubs around me. It wasn't the garden that I'd imagined as a child, one lush with flowers and bushes like an elaborate English estate. This place felt dingy and dusty, and there were few flowers.

I shivered as the sun started to set, and the air grew noticeably cooler. I walked alone, avoiding my travel companions, wanting to be in this space on my own terms, not chatting or even listening to others.

*Did that verse in Matthew have anything to teach me? What cup was I holding, and what did I need to let go?* I replayed in my head the life motto conversation we'd had over dinner with our host family, still regretting that I'd shared something so personal but also knowing I wanted to live more like I had in that moment. To be able to be real about life, and not pretend or feel ashamed for being genuine. This internal tug of war between my empathic self and the intellectual non-feeling self was becoming a battle of wills.

We returned to the bus, and I stared out the window as the bus made its way through narrow streets to the Western Wall, where people wrote their prayers on little paper slips and tucked their prayers into the wall of rocks. I had some serious prayers I wanted to make, most of all for my friend John who was still struggling to stay ahead of his cancer. But I felt uncomfortable participating in a ritual that wasn't mine. *Would my prayers be welcome at this Jewish place?* I recalled TV images of people dressed in black, sticking notes into the cracks, weeping and bowing before the stone slabs, and looking very foreign to my young Catholic eyes.

We walked up the hill towards the gates. There were long lines to enter, with separate entrances for women and men. Stuffing my hands into my pockets, I walked a few steps behind the others as we slowly made our way through the gate. Hundreds of people milled about the expansive plaza and I joined the masses, slipping through those dressed in black coats and long dresses towards the towering wall. A solid line of people stood before it, faces pressed against the stone. There was no room for me, and I didn't have a prayer slip to stick in the crack. I reached out my hand and found a spot between two women where I could touch its cool surface and bow my head, silently saying my prayers.

I backed away from the wall as more women gently pushed to take the place of anyone who left. I didn't want to leave, but I didn't want to just stand there looking at the wall with its line of people pressed against it like a row of shrubs. White plastic chairs like those I had at home were scattered around the plaza. I sat down, wrapping my coat tight around me, and pulling my scarf higher on my neck. I leaned over and placed my elbows on my knees, resting my chin in my hands. I glanced around at the mass of people, the wads of white paper sticking out of the wall, and the sea of black. I thought of John and the others on my imaginary prayer slips, of my life motto, and how I'd made myself so vulnerable on this trip. My head dropped, and I covered my face with my hands as my eyes burned. I blinked hard. I did not want to cry in public. I lifted my head for a second to make sure none of the other women from our group could see me. My tears simply could not be stopped. I pressed my fingers into my eyes, hoping to push them back inside, but they just flowed uncontrollably. Rocking my shoulders back and forth, I waited for the sobs to end. I peeked out between my fingers, watching as stockinged legs and black-clad feet walk past. I wondered if they knew I was a Catholic—an interloper wailing at their wall?

I focused on the ground, not wanting to lift my face, knowing it was red, blotchy, and puffy from crying. I inhaled the cold night air, trying to regain my composure. After a few minutes, I lifted my head and looked up at the top of the wall, as if the answers could be seen above in the inky black sky.

*What am I supposed to be doing? Why am I crying?*

Shivering in the cold air, I closed my eyes and heard a voice say clearly:

*Speak your truth. Let your light shine.*

I looked back up at the wall, expecting some person to be perched on top of the wall with their hands cupped around their mouth, whispering those words to me. Yet, I only saw the wall of limestone and infinite sky. I blinked my eyes again and looked around. *Did I really hear that? This is crazy—is it a joke? Some trick to make me believe, or a prank to remind me it was all fake?*

I remembered a bible verse about how we aren't supposed to put our light under a bushel basket. Light was meant to shine. I thought of my blunder just two nights before, when I shared my life motto and its origin. I had definitely spoken my truth. I tried to shake off the voice I'd heard as just a crazy inner thought wanting validation. It was all in my head. But those words stuck with me like the prayers suspended in the wall.

*eleven*

---

# Hitting Bottom

few months after the business trip to Israel, I sat in my office shamelessly scrolling through jobs on a nonprofit job board. Part-time grants management with a small nonprofit—that sounded tempting. Executive director of a workforce development organization—I could do that. Advocacy coordinator for a children's organization—sure thing. Other listings piqued my interest, but I closed out of the page without saving any of them.

"You should hire a career coach," my friend told me. "I know a few. I'll send some information to you."

Maybe that would help. God knows I spent plenty of money on years of therapy to achieve my current level of insanity. I could probably use some outside help again.

I'd never had any career guidance before, or at least none that I had sought out.

"With your grades, you should apply to Harvard and Vassar," one teacher told me.

"Your ACT score should get you into most any college," the guidance counselor stated matter-of-factly.

"Have you considered becoming a nun?" one religious person asked.

"You'd be a great teacher."

"What about social work?"

"You could be a doctor or lawyer," others suggested.

No one had asked what I really *wanted* to do. And now in my 40s I still didn't have an answer to that question. But I was no longer able to follow anyone's advice. Stage four melanoma had put an end to my blind obedience.

I looked around my spacious office with its window overlooking a parking lot that often show-cased military helicopters and bombers from the museum next door and sighed. In my job, I'd been placating demanding partners and putting out internal fires, while being accused of creating a toxic work environment by a disgruntled employee who was unhappy with her sub-par performance review. I knew I was just repeating the same pattern when I said yes to the original interview question years before— taking whatever came at me. I stared at my title on my business cards stacked in the wooden holder by my computer, wondering what it all meant. A huge calendar hung on the wall with all my meetings and travel dates penciled in, color-coded by project.

My job was everything I had dreamed of, so why did I want to walk away and never come back?

*Because you're a crazy loon,* I told myself.

*Because you don't want to die as a group director.*

Who was right?

I followed my friend's advice and contacted a career coach who sent me a form to complete, which included questions about your purpose in life and secret passions. The questions spoke to me as I felt my career quest wasn't just about climbing a ladder or finding the right industry, but about answering those deeper inquiries about purpose and passion. The minute I hit send, I felt relief.

In our second meeting, I tried answering the questions about purpose and what I'd really like to do and stumbled over my words. The coach interrupted me, "Do you realize how often you say 'I don't know?'"

I looked at her quizzically. "What do you mean?"

"You were just starting to say something, and you trailed off with 'I don't know' and then you stopped."

"Really?"

"Yes. You do it a lot."

"Huh."

I restated my previous thought, "I think I should be able to resign by the end of May, but I don't know . . . I have three big meetings to organize in June. But then there's our annual summer meeting in August. I'm in charge of an important conference in September."

I rattled off the big blocks of time on my calendar and the list of to-dos.

"See. You said you'd like to resign in May, and then you said 'I don't know' because of all those excuses you gave."

*Shit!* She was right.

I sat, letting it sink in for a minute, and wondered what would happen if I were to quit at the end of the month. My anxiety rose like water filling a tub, and I soon felt as if I was drowning in the idea of leaving my obligations unfilled. I couldn't do it. What was I thinking?

She looked at me square in the eyes, "What would you do if you left?"

Without hesitation, "I'd write. But I don't know . . . what do I have to say?"

"You did it again."

*Damn!* I threw my head back, slapping my pen onto the notebook in my lap.

"I don't know," I sighed.

"I think you do know. Finish your sentence."

I looked at her, then down at my hands, skimming my notes and remembering what I wrote on the first questionnaire she asked me to fill out.

"I would write, and hike, and spend my time outdoors." I fought back the "I don't know" crawling up my throat. I wanted to cover up the audacity of my wishes with some logical or pragmatic idea, like consulting or finding some other job.

Those words hung there, and I wanted to grab them and shove them back into a bottle like they were an escaped genie.

"How did it feel saying that?"

"Crazy, like—who am I to think I can do that?" After a deep breath I added, "But freeing as well. It's the only answer I have right now. It makes no sense, but it's what keeps coming up."

Images of that night at the Wailing Wall in Jerusalem flashed in front of me, as the voice repeated its mantra. *Speak your truth. Shine your light.* I could not shut it up. It kept whispering to me and I kept shushing it, even while feeling hopeful about the freedom it declared.

"Tell me what you would write about."

"I don't know . . . "

"Eh," she interrupted.

I took another deep breath and sat up straighter in the cushy rocking chair. "I would write a book. About survival. I've read so many cancer books by great authors, but they die. I want to write a book about surviving. What I've learned. I want to inspire others to live, truly live." And I went on and on about my dreams of writing a book and my title ideas.

"Did you see yourself relax as you talked about that?"

"No, not really."

"I just watched your entire body soften. Your neck and shoulders loosened."

I looked down at my hands, which were no longer clutching the pen and notebook but sitting loosely on my lap. I felt myself held by the chair as my body relaxed into its softness. The sting of a tear formed in my eyes, as I finally realized the power of my words.

We sat in silence while I absorbed the feelings of freedom and of watching my dreams come to life.

"I really do need to leave," I told her.

When and how to leave remained the questions—but wasn't that why I sought out a career coach in the first place? To answer the question of whether to stay or go.

Even though I wanted this answer, I knew I needed much more than that. I needed to figure out how.

A month later in the career coach's office, I was barely in the door when she asked, "Did you submit your resignation?"

Unable to face her, I looked down, pretending to grab something from my bag as I sat down in the chair.

"No," I answered. "I just couldn't bring myself to do it," I commented, slumping in the chair as I remembered our breakthrough conversation, my dreams of leaving, and the freedom of walking away. And my commitment that I would leave.

"Why not?"

"I don't know. Maybe it's not that bad. They finally cleared me of the harassment charge."

Even though I had expected that outcome, it really did feel like a win, considering the other job conditions that I agreed to follow. I was clinging to anything positive, hoping it would expose the absurdity of wanting to leave this prestigious and well-paying position.

I sat, saying nothing for a few minutes.

"How does this change your original desire to resign?"

"I guess it makes it a little easier to stay," I replied, my voice trailed off as I imagined continuing in the job without a backstabbing colleague.

She watched me as I played the same movie over in my head, patiently waiting for me to change the script.

"It doesn't really change anything," I finally admitted. "I can't figure out why I can't do this."

"What do you think you need?"

"Some reassurance that I'll make it. That I'm not crazy. That I'll be able to pay the bills." Many other fears rambled out of my mouth. I kept talking in circles. I gave her a new date for my resignation. We set another appointment for 2 weeks later, and I knew she'd hold me to my promise. I still wasn't sure I was good for it yet.

---

An email came on a Monday morning at the office. The subject line included just a colleague's name. I knew the news would be bad; she had been sick and I knew her cancer was progressing. Another coworker was dying on the job. Another person who had a better prognosis, but who'd landed on the other side of the odds.

Nine days later, my colleagues slowly filed into the funeral home, all dressed in navy or black suits and skirts. I gazed down at my black pants and wrapped my thin black shawl tighter around my body.

This was the fifth funeral I'd attended since my diagnosis, the third for a coworker. My mind constantly swapped the person in the casket for me, and swapped mourning colleagues for my own family. I was flipping back and forth between two channels, trying to watch two shows at once.

Alan's uncle had died first of lung cancer, 5 months after my diagnosis. We shared some tender moments in the brief time that I knew him. He was a sweet man, and we connected easily. His service was on a Monday morning. I had rushed to the funeral home to attend, and then sped back to my house just in time to grab my baggy pants and pick up my sister who would accompany me for that week's treatment. From funeral home to hospital bed. I cried as much for myself as for Alan's uncle.

Two months later, I sat in a packed Presbyterian church for a funeral of a coworker's husband. He had died of stage four melanoma. The cancer had gone to his brain. I didn't know my coworker well, but we found ourselves walking similar paths on different sides of the trail. I squeezed myself into a back pew and hoped no one would see me sobbing for someone I did not know. Tears of guilt flowed for surviving the same disease, and knowing that I could never fill a church as he did.

Just a few weeks later, my grandmother left this earthly world after 94 years of gracing my life with her dry humor and feisty spirit. My family asked me to deliver one of the bible readings at her funeral mass. Having recently completed treatments and been given the all-clear, I still looked like hell. My pale sickly face and long stringy hair hadn't been cut in months, and I felt eyes on me as I walked up to the altar, wondering how many whispered, "Is she the one who was *really* sick?" I held back the lump in my throat, and managed to read the verse without crying. I returned to my pew, passing my grandmother's coffin and realizing many of these same people would be here if I were lying in the casket. I slid in beside Alan and grabbed his hand. My aunt sitting behind us put her hand on my back, likely a thank you for reading. Her gesture released my thoughts of gratitude for living. My tears flowed freely.

The day that I had returned to the office after my grandmother's funeral, my former boss died. He had been in the hospital dealing with new complications, but I never expected to get the news so quickly. We had talked the day I left for Iowa, for my grandmother's funeral. He had been scheduled to go on a trip, and told me he wouldn't be able to go. I didn't think much of it, but something seemed off when I said goodbye as he remained silent instead of saying his usual send-off, "Goodbye, Rochelle." He had to have known it would be his last goodbye; I think he wasn't ready to verbalize and acknowledge that truth.

His death brought a sense of loss, along with questions about how I wanted to live, and a reminder that my health sat in the balance. At his funeral, I stood before my colleagues and delivered a short eulogy. Afterwards, I vowed not to die on the job or—heaven forbid—be memorialized in the same room where we held all-staff meetings.

So here I was 3 years after his death, sitting at yet another funeral service, surrounded again by colleagues as we bowed our heads and listened to the rabbi speak about my peer and her life legacy. The usual thoughts swirled through my mind—why was I in the pew and not in the casket? Looking around, I saw many familiar faces, people I would see in the office on the stairwell or in the breakroom. Some I'd run with during lunchtime jaunts; others I'd shared glasses of wine with at conference receptions. I didn't know most of the attendees, who were presumably family members as well as plenty of professional colleagues. I spotted a few local elected officials and education experts.

My colleague's bereaved husband stood up, and moved towards the front of the room. He had a radio announcer's voice and perfect articulation as he shared stories about their travels and biking adventures. The stories brought her back to life as I imagined them riding mountain passes together, year after year, enjoying the hundreds of miles on a bike with a group of friends. He drew a picture of her that I'd not witnessed firsthand—of a carefree and adventurous woman who liked to cook.

I wish that I had known her.

One of her team members stood up and spoke with deep admiration and love for the boss who had treated her like a daughter. I pictured them sitting in the kitchen, sharing a meal and glass of wine, the image so incongruent with the business-like veneer she portrayed in the office.

It's amazing how different people can be outside their work worlds.

If it were my funeral, would one of my staff stand up and extol my virtues, or speak eloquently about me having any influence or impact on their life? The thought unnerved me. I didn't want my coworkers to outnumber my family and personal friends. I didn't want an email to go out to the company, informing my professional colleagues I was dying.

As we drove back to the office after the funeral, I sat in the back seat while two of my colleagues sat in the front. They talked about upcoming meetings without mentioning anything about the service, or our colleague who had just passed. I looked out the window, fighting back tears, wishing I could just get out and walk alone. When we pulled up to the stop light, the hearse drove alongside us; the name of the funeral parlor in curving calligraphy on the tinted back window. I watched it slowly pass, and saw the casket behind the dark glass. Her body was in there. The tan and lean body that I had visited just days ago was now permanently encased and soon to be interred in the ground. Her death became real in that moment. As did my own.

I bit my lip. This was *not* the time to cry. My coworkers were *not* people I wanted to cry in front of. I knew my tears were not for my former colleague. I was riding in my own hearse, trapped inside a casket I had made for myself, going to the office that was slowly suffocating the real life out of me.

---

During my previous session 6 weeks ago, my career coach asked when I was going to submit my letter of resignation. I had responded confidently that May 31st would be my last day.

It was now June as I sat in the coach's office, and I still hadn't followed through on my promise. The letter was written—hell, I had dreamed of the letter years ago, and had written a first draft months ago. Yet the words remained in my laptop, waiting for me to pull them out of cyberspace and the subconscious world and make them real.

"So, what kept you from giving your notice this week?"

Her words cut through my overachieving, follow-through-on-everything self. I always prided myself on delivering on my promises, responding to people in a timely manner, doing what I said I would do.

Stabs of guilt and shame turned into jabs of excuses and self-defense.

I rattled off my upcoming meetings and deadlines. I whined about the reports I knew were due; about timing, and how busy the summer was; and how I could put up with the job for a few more months. Besides, I needed to figure out insurance, and what to do with the vacation I had planned.

"Huh," was all she said.

I kept on rambling, hoping to somehow convince her that I still wanted to leave—that I would follow through on my promise, but I just couldn't do it right now. It was clear that the person who needed persuasion was not her, but me.

"Have you changed your mind? You don't want to leave the job after all?"

*Ugh.* I wanted to stomp my feet and scream *No!* I hadn't changed my mind—I just couldn't do it. I couldn't look at her. I stared at my hands. I found it nearly impossible to fight against the messages that I'd been listening to all my life and the demands to be perfect and achieve. The message I received that day on the farm when everyone told me how helpful I was. The message I received when my sister Jolene was sick, and I had stepped up to take care of my little sisters. The message I received in high school said if I built a wall around myself, I would be safe. The belief that better job titles and higher salaries reflected my worth. The messages I thought that saved me from my pain but seemed to cause even more suffering.

*Crap! Why does she push my buttons like this?*

"What are you thinking?" She asked, breaking the silence and my internal argument.

"Just how fricking frustrating it is that I can't make a decision. That I can't do this."

I sighed and studied my fingers, noticing the brown freckles and veins protruding on my pale wrists.

"What would it feel like if you did it; if you actually gave your notice?"

I looked up at her and took a deep breath.

"It would be liberating. I'd be free of this superficial world. I could stop pretending I care or that I don't care, and I could stop being afraid to stand up for myself."

My nagging belief that my job stress was impacting my health reminded me of the signs my body gave me about the cost of those choices. The walls I built did *not* protect me. And my pleasing and perfecting ways did *not* make me immune to disease. In fact, it probably caused it! The internal tug of war that quietly took place without my awareness became real on that day driving to Bryce Canyon. My body was sick of fighting, and every tumor, the mammogram abnormality, the fibroid in my ovary, were all reminders that I was *not* living in alignment. I believed that to be true, feeling that the stress I tried to ignore still did its damage. And even as I rose to a higher leadership position in my job, I was still bending over backwards and compromising my true self. I wanted to be the woman I discovered in that canyon, the person I was with John and Janice, and the person I was at the dinner table in Jerusalem offering her life motto. I wanted to be fully alive and wholly human. My gut longed to leave.

I imagined myself not going into my office. Not having to schmooze, or play politics, or bend over backwards for people. No suits. No conference rooms or ballroom receptions. No smiling and nodding; no rushing to put out fires or analyzing every single word or sentence for perfect political balance. No more babysitting or cheerleading.

I imagined trails opening before me. Mountains stood in the distance, waiting to be climbed. Waiting to welcome me into their forested embrace and carry me to their rocky summits. The fresh air filling my lungs as I imagined the freedom of being outside.

Finally, I could write and figure out what the hell had happened in my life these last 4 years. Possibly figure out what the heck I was supposed to be doing with these bonus days? This bonus life? Maybe answer the question of why I'm still alive while others aren't? Why did I get the lucky 5-percent ticket? Do I have a larger purpose?

My very first interview with my organization and their warning about my boss played out in my head. The specific instructions to *not* complain. That they knew they had a problem but were not willing to fix it. I had no idea when I accepted those terms what it would mean to accept that challenge and the rules. I had established myself as the loyal employee, willing to gamely tackle whatever was put in front of me, and to work around whatever barrier was in my way, until a disgruntled employee accused me of creating a toxic work environment. The irony of that experience dealt a fatal blow to my firmly held belief that my loyalty would always be rewarded and safeguarded. The only person who could take care of me was *me*. I was finally going to walk away from the lousy deal they handed me. I would say no to their rules and expectations, and not allow them to take advantage of my agreeable nature, my compliance, my people-pleasing self-sacrificing ways.

"Do you know what just happened to your body as you talked about that?" she asked.

"Umm, no." I looked down again, and didn't see anything obviously different.

"Your whole body relaxed. I saw your neck muscles and veins just vanish. Your eyes are brighter. Your jaw wasn't as clenched."

I looked back at her, and tried to focus on my neck and jaw. I rolled my shoulders and opened my mouth. The motions felt easy. I took a deep breath and settled into the cushion, allowing the rest of my body to settle into the velvety fabric.

"Yes, it would feel pretty damn good," I smiled. I had the same feeling of relief I'd experienced during our previous conversations when I pictured myself leaving my job.

Free. Alive. Me. That's who I would be. The same woman who said, *Fuck you, doctor, I'm going to live.* That's who I'd be. My own person doing what I love, to heck with society's expectations. I could imagine what it would feel like, but I struggled to let go.

Oh, how I wanted to be that person! How I wished I had been that person for the first 40 years of my life. Where would I be if I could say no instead of always saying yes?

"So, what do you need to make this happen?" my coach asked.

"I wish I knew. There's still a part of me that doesn't want to leave. It's probably the money. This is the most money I've ever made."

Which was true, and a big deal. I had grown up with hand-me-downs and free lunches. My family couldn't afford name-brand clothing, and I had started working as a teenager so I could buy a pair of Nike basketball shoes and ditch the generic shoes I wore. I'd been saving 40 percent of my income since I was 26 years old. I had padded a nice savings account, a sizeable retirement fund, and I was married. But I was reluctant to let Alan pay for everything. I wanted to be a self-sufficient self-made woman. I had paid for nearly everything in my life since those first pair of shoes. Now, I could even buy things without doing high-level math to determine if it was going to break my budget. Having money was a huge accomplishment—a validation of my worth. And it was an escape from the constant stress and stigma of driving beat-up cars or wearing cheap clothes.

Would I end up pinching pennies again? I shuddered to think about the embarrassment I felt, walking into the church rectory to collect my free lunch ticket from the mean lunch lady who looked at me like I was a beggar on the street. I tried to stretch my 10-day ticket for as long as possible, saving the punches for pizza, or when I was really hungry and couldn't fathom how I'd get through basketball practice after school without eating. I never wanted anyone to look at me like that again.

I was afraid of letting the money, and all it meant, go. It was another protection that I had used to shield myself from pain, but was starting to feel more like a cage keeping me from being free. I wanted to walk away, without a job in hand, to go write or hike or just do nothing for a change. I wanted just to live.

Pure selfishness, some might say. Others might laugh at my salary, and wonder why I thought this was some million-dollar job I was leaving. Whether it was a lot of money or not enough, I imagined others wondering why I would ever give up a paycheck at all, much less one that I'd dreamed of having.

My dreams clearly had changed. My desire to do something else with my life outweighed my want of a paycheck. I was good at what I did, but there were other things I felt compelled to do. I knew that just because we're good at something does not mean it's our destiny. Passions change. We are not still ponds or pools of stagnant water but flowing rivers. Life moves along, and we change. Like water carving out exquisite canyons over time, new layers of ourselves are revealed over time and our struggles, digging deeper into our souls. My illness felt more like a flash flood gouging an old riverbed, and unlocking huge boulders that tumbled down the canyon exposing a whole new rock bottom, widening its path, and destroying whatever got in its way.

I was still trying to put those boulders back in place. Still acting like the flood never happened. Afraid to build anew with the raw material now exposed and littered across the floor. Could I ever accept the destruction of the old, and carve a new path?

*twelve*

—

# Standing Up

I can't get the screw to come out. It's not a Phillips," I said to Janice, my body contorting and twisting underneath the vanity as I tried to release the screw so we could remove it from the wall. "It's one of those square heads. Maybe an Allen wrench would work."

"Oh, OK," Janice sighed. "Well, we don't have any more time as John has to be at the radiology clinic soon."

Right. The real reason for my visit was not to work on home improvement projects, but to provide a little breathing room for John's wife. His wife who handled stress by tearing down walls and ripping out bathroom cabinets.

It was a week after my recent session with the career coach, and I was still fighting the desire to resign and my stubborn will to make my job work for me. But John was my priority, so my work woes took a back seat.

"I can try again when we get back."

I brushed the dust off my pants and walked downstairs where John was seated in the high-back chair.

"So, who's taking me to my appointment?" he asked, looking at Janice.

"I am. We'll let Janice continue her bathroom demolition project." I teased.

"Oh. Well, we better get going." I could sense a little discomfort as he realized I would be his chauffeur. It felt a little strange to me as well. I was simply a fellow cancer patient who had befriended this kind and gentle man a few years prior. We'd spent hours swapping stories and talking about everything from cancer treatments to midwestern traditions and attending bluegrass concerts. I never imagined our friendship would include taking him to a radiation appointment. I had only envisioned continued celebratory dinners and gratitude notes about how lucky we both were to respond to IL-2 and survive this insidious disease. I didn't expect to be a witness and close companion on his final journey.

But I couldn't leave him now. I couldn't ignore the reality of his prognosis, or leave his wife and kids who had so graciously welcomed a random stranger and her husband into their lives. We had come too far, gone through too much, and shared too many memories.

I wanted him to get better. I wanted the treatments to work like the previous drugs. I wanted another miracle for him and for his family. Yet, I knew the odds were not good. There were complications and a continued progression of the disease. I knew eventually it would be too much for his body, despite his strength of mind and hopeful attitude. It broke my heart in ways I'd never felt before. To see him go through what I had feared—and what I knew could happen to me, like watching a movie preview.

We walked to the car in silence, and I watched as he slowly lifted his leg and lowered himself into my little Honda Civic. His knee was so close to mine, closer than we'd ever sat together. His 6-foot frame filled the passenger seat, and he reached across his shoulder to grab the seat belt. I put my hand on the gear shifter, now just inches from his thigh. His long legs were crammed into the space; he didn't bother to move his leg and my fingers brushed his knee a few times as I shifted gears. I wanted to put my hand on his thigh, and give it a comforting squeeze.

"Turn here, and we'll take the scenic route," he instructed.

"Sounds good."

I drove, wondering what to say. We were alone. No spouses to distract us, or dominate the conversation. Just me and my melanoma warrior, the moniker he coined for us. I wished I wasn't escorting him to a new battlefield. A battle I feared that he was losing, and I think we both knew it. No words seemed right. We drove in silence.

I pulled into the hospital parking lot. He took slow and deliberate steps across the pavement and into the lobby, waving to the receptionist as we walked past.

"Hi John. Back for another treatment?"

"Yup."

This wasn't his first trip. He clearly knew where he was going, and people knew him.

"She is a cancer survivor too," nodding towards me as he looked back to the sweet receptionist.

"Ahh," she smiled back at me.

I smiled back. Aren't we all, I thought?

I looked around, trying to get my bearings in this new place. None of my treatments or doctor visits had brought me to this building. Radiation had never made it on my to-do list. I suddenly felt grateful as the smell of sickness and hospital stifled the air, bringing nauseating memories with every breath.

John led me back to the waiting area, and sat down in the chair next to the table with a stack of magazines. I settled in next to him; our legs and shoulders nearly touching. I felt his body heat; life pulsing through his long arms and legs, and I wondered how much time he had left on this earth. I wanted to lean into his shoulder, but I crossed my hands across my stomach and kept rehearsing the words that hung in the back of my throat, unable to break through my tightened jaw.

"They take me back to a little room . . . ." John explained the process, and I tried to listen to what he was saying as I fought with the tangle of thoughts that I wanted to express. The receptionist was a cancer survivor too. She had been nice to him, and gave him some tips. Patient to patient, like he had done for me. He always had a way of finding connections with people. I was happy that he had someone to guide his path as he had done for me, and felt guilty I couldn't offer him anything but a silent ride.

The waiting area was empty; a perfect time to tell him how I felt. But telling him what he meant to me would only acknowledge the finality of our days together, and weren't we supposed to remain hopeful? Weren't we both supposed to ride this melanoma tail to infinity? I felt the camaraderie we shared drifting away, like a leaf flowing downstream as I stood on the shore watching it float into the distance. The words wouldn't leave my broken heart. I rehearsed them over and over again, as I looked around at the pastel wall paintings.

"Thank you for bringing me," he said, breaking the silence.

Those simple words broke a tiny piece of my heart.

"You're welcome." I reached over and put my hand on his arm. "You have had a tremendous impact on my life, John. I want you to know that. I am so grateful for you."

He looked down at my hand and nodded, then placed his other hand on mine.

"Thank you."

It was all that would come out, even though I wanted to say so much more. To tell him how his journey shaped mine. I wanted to wrap my arms around him and somehow make the truth of his illness go away. I wanted to pretend that we were just waiting to see the doctor who'd tell him he was going to be fine. That the radiation was working. That his weakness and difficulty walking would improve. I wanted him to get better. I squeezed his arm, hoping all those wishes would shoot out through my fingertips into his flesh and up to his heart. I wanted him to know just how much I loved him, how much he had given me. I gave him one long squeeze.

"John, we're ready for you now."

I looked up to see the radiology tech smiling as she waited, and he slowly pushed himself up from the chair. He looked down at me, his eyes looking straight in mine, the same blue eyes that had stared in mine as we had shared stories of hallucinations, belly injections, hope, and gratitude.

"I'll be right back," he said, a reassuring smile on his face.

---

About a month later, I pedaled my bicycle as hard as I could, hoping that every light would be green as I sped along the street. The skies could open at any moment, and I needed to get to the hospital. I turned into the driveway and jumped off my bike, propping it against the house. I swung my backpack around, so I could get the garage door opener out of the side pocket and waited impatiently for it to rise. I hurried through the door as my beagle came to greet me.

"Mama's got to go. I'm so sorry. I'll be back," I said, petting him and walking him to the back door to let him out. He burst out and circled the yard, while I scurried to the bedroom and ripped off my biking shorts and sweaty shirt. I unzipped my pack and put my skirt and sweater back on, not wanting to waste time finding something else to wear. My hair was in a ponytail, now damp with perspiration. I couldn't go like this. I pulled out the hairband and tried to comb out the ponytail bump and total flat top. John is dying, I thought. He doesn't care about my hair.

I spritzed some perfume on my neck, then grabbed my keys and a water bottle as I encouraged Junior to come back inside. His tail wagging, I bent down to give him a kiss as he looked up wondering why I wasn't staying. I cooed at him and pointed to his dog dish, reassuring him that I'd be back soon as I shut the door behind me.

I sped down the interstate, grateful that the traffic was moving along nicely. As I pulled into the hospital parking lot, I finally took a breath. I looked up at the big brick building and sighed. John was in one of those rooms.

I walked briskly to the front lobby as light rain dampened my already sweaty head. The receptionist gave me directions, and I walked to the elevator and pressed the button, grateful it had 5 floors to descend as I tried to catch my breath, turn off work brain, and focus on life.

I was anxious to see my friend, but also wishing that the elevator would never open so I could stay within its tiny four walls by myself like a cocoon. I kept rehearsing words and trying to imagine what to say to my dear friends—one of whom was dying—the other who was doing her best to survive.

The doors opened, and I walked towards the nurse's station, and then found his room.

"John, what are you doing in here again?" I teased as I walked towards his bed, his wife smiling at me from her usual spot in the chair next to him.

"I missed the food," he said, his familiar sly grin stretching across his face. Janice laughed. We all knew she was a great cook.

I sat down in the other chair at the foot of the bed, as they explained what was going on, the plan, and the treatments. John always knew every drug name, and the latest research concerning what it did, its side effects, and effectiveness. I nodded as if I knew what he was talking about, feeling guilty I did not. I didn't need to pay attention because my scans continued to be clear.

I watched as they spoke calmly of the current situation, seeing the exhaustion in their eyes. Another setback. My heart broke as I felt the love and hope mixing with fear and desperation while their options kept dwindling. No one wanted to be in that room.

---

I followed John's passages from hospital rooms to a skilled nursing facility as he continued to try whatever treatment might help. The summer days were hazy with death clouds looming. Work projects kept my mind distracted, or perhaps just agitated by the pointless nature of my job. I made some mistakes that I blamed on my conflicted mind, questioning everything, and caring about nothing other than living, and living well.

I knew I could have been facing the same set of dwindling options as John. I knew I could be lying in a hospital bed, while Alan perched in one of those uncomfortable chairs watching me die in front of him. I put myself in John's shoes, in that bed, and it broke my heart to watch this sweet man who called himself Lucky Johnny, who wrote notes about *getting* to shovel snow—and watching hope, life, and joy be slowly drained away. To witness the love between a husband and a wife during these final days, a testament to the human spirit demonstrating the humanity of death, and the ability to continue with everyday life.

---

I received a text from Janice on a Tuesday night. *You might want to come over tonight to say goodbye.*

I clutched my phone to my chest, hoping it would keep my heart from jumping out of my body. I knew his death was coming, but no amount of knowing makes you prepared for what it feels like when it happens. The air stopped moving and my shoulders sank as I tried to create a container for my grief—to somehow hold it in my lap. I pictured him with his eyes closed, breathing his last breaths, his physical body slowly letting go until all that remained was his spirit.

No more John jokes or sweet notes of encouragement. Everything that he meant to me flashed before me in a kaleidoscope of color and light. And then it went dark. I suddenly realized *I* was losing him.

All this time I had been so worried about him, how was he handling the facts of his illness and the certainty of his death. How was he coping with the vision of his wife left alone, without him? How much pain was he experiencing? What words did he still want to say? How can one say all of that to everyone? I wondered about all the thoughts I might have if I were in his situation. I had spent the last few months in his shoes and those of his family. That night, I finally realized I had my own grief to wear.

I was losing him—my person. The only other human who could fully relate to what I had experienced. The only person who walked this narrow path, balancing on 5- to 7-percent odds and slim margins. The only person who knew the fear and worry that comes with every PET scan. The only person who also found a gift in their diagnosis.

The enormity of the void swallowed me in its silence and loneliness. What was I going to do without him? How would I know what all those polysyllabic medical terms and research statistics mean without my melanoma scientist? How would I know if my symptoms and crazy phantom pains are real or normal? Who would celebrate with me when I get a clean scan? Who would high-five me when I hit the 5-year milestone? And who would look into my eyes, see straight through to my soul, and speak volumes without uttering a word? His eyes blue, like pools of glass deep as an ocean and soft as the sea.

We went to his house where they had set up a hospital bed in the living room. I cried ugly tears, blubbering all the things that I wanted to say that night at the radiology clinic. I held his soft hands, feeling the silky smooth of his warm skin, rubbing my palm on his wrist as my tears fell onto the edge of the bed. I couldn't bear to leave him and all that we shared—where we had first met in person; where we had shared meals; our deep connection despite our 20-plus-year age difference. I leaned down, placing my head on his chest and hugged him tight, thanking him for bringing so much hope and joy to my life.

I stood and hugged Janice, allowing her to comfort me, instead of me comforting her. She knew what John meant to me without having to say a word. My heart broke in her arms.

John died two days later. I received the news minutes after I had arrived at my office. I shut the door and stared out the window at the parking lot, trying to imagine my life without him. Scanning the asphalt lot, my eyes were drawn to the vacant space normally occupied by my colleague who just passed, in addition to the spot where my former boss used to park. I inhaled deeply, closing my eyes.

The next day, I was at my desk when I heard a knock on the door.

"Did you hear the news about the project?" my coworker asked urgently.

"No. What news is that?" I inquired. Staying abreast of the latest office happenings was not my strong suit. I tended to be the last to know about most gossip.

"They gave it to Linda."

A fire lit in my belly as I recalled the sacrifices I'd made for the company. This project was one I had always wanted to lead. Being assigned that project might have been the one thing to keep me in my job.

I then imagined John lying in his hospital bed, and knew that it could've been me. We had the same disease, the same prognosis. Many of the same treatments. But he had loved his job; my colleague had loved her job. I hadn't loved my job for a few years. As much as I wanted to hold onto my identity and role as a high-achieving professional, I could no longer ignore this nudge to find a new path. It was time to let go.

"I'm not surprised," I responded.

My coworker looked at me with wild eyes, ready to fight for me.

"It's OK. Really."

I knew what I needed to do. I finalized my resignation letter that had been sitting dormant on my computer and printed it off. Signing my name felt as terrifying and liberating as when I bought my first house. This time, however, I wasn't committing to a bank or a building, but was investing in myself. And finally saying, *No, I will not have another*.

John's death had confirmed my gut feelings that it was time to move on and start over. I didn't want to die in the role I was playing, I knew that for sure. What exactly I wanted to do before I died remained unclear, but now I was definitely committed to find out or die trying.

Finally, I walked into the CEO's office and handed him my resignation. Over the following days and weeks, he and others tried to convince me to stay, but I refused their bids to keep me, as tempting as they were. This time I did not succumb to their offers, or twist and bend to meet their demands. Instead, I chose to stand tall and hold my ground.

---

I kept looking at my watch, hoping the speaker would wrap up the meeting so I could get out of my suit and onto the trail. It was my final meeting with this group, and I spent much of the time informing people I was leaving. I'm not sure what I expected, perhaps encouragement and maybe even a job offer; something to say my time there had been valued. Instead, I mostly received questions about who would take over my job responsibilities, and who they should contact.

I squirmed in my seat as the organizer gave her final remarks. She asked a young woman to come up to the mic. She had written a heartfelt poem about connection and family, building bridges, and creating community, and the pain of injustice and struggle. Her words pulled me in like a fish hooked on a line, as her prose spoke to the deeper reason why I had ever sat at this table in my suit.

I'd been working on social policy issues because I cared about people and families, and especially those who struggled. I did it under the cover of my suit, disguising my heart with intellectual debates and bullet-point lists of policy pros and cons. I believed the suit opened doors and magically conferred power and prestige. I walked proudly through state capitols, down D.C. streets and through ballrooms filled with policy elites feeling strong, confident, professional, and in control. I'd traded the messiness of social work for sterile suits and stuffy meeting rooms. My desire for justice turned into neutral briefs filled with technical jargon.

But the suit never fulfilled its original purpose of shielding me from the heart of life. It was merely a costume I wore to enter the party, to sit at the power table and pretend to make a difference. The heart I'd been running from had busted through the jacket's buttons the day I was diagnosed. I thought I could tuck her safely back into the neat and tidy black outfit, but she oozed from every seam and longed to be set free. The suit no longer fit me. And without it, I no longer belonged at that table.

While disappointed by callous and selfish reactions to my departure, I felt more peaceful than I had in a long time. I looked up at the young woman reading her poem as she put her heart out there, silently thanking her for modeling the messy and calling forth the inspired. After she spoke her final words, I walked briskly to the table with the box lunches, grabbing the first cardboard container and walking out the door, not looking back as I headed straight to my car.

I shifted the car into reverse, and quickly maneuvered out of the parking lot and through the windy streets, and headed up the pass. I unbuckled my belt and untucked my shirt as I drove my way up the narrow highway pass. The aspens were mostly bare, but a few golden leaves flickered in the late morning sun. Clouds were building, and I hit the gas as much as I could on the curvy two-lane road.

I swung into a parking lot, thankful to see just one other car. My overnight bag sat unzipped on the opposite seat, my running gear on top. I slipped off my heels and threw them on the passenger seat floor, quickly slid my pants down around my ankles and reached down, my cheek pushed against the steering wheel as I strained to grab my pants and toss them on the back seat. I grabbed my running tights and bent down to punch my ankles through the tiny openings. I sat with my bare thighs and pink bikini underwear, looking around to make sure no one could see me as a truck came slowly around the bend. Luckily, it was just a cautious mountain driver who continued snaking up the pass. I lifted my hips and swiftly pulled up my tights. I had been smart enough to put my sports bra on that morning, so I could just pull my dress shirt over my head and replace it with my favorite running shirt.

I opened the door, and put on my socks and shoes. I grabbed my waist belt with water bottle and phone, tossed on my vest, and slipped on my hat and gloves. It was a few minutes after noon. I had 1 hour and 28 minutes to run. I locked the door, stashed my keys in my pocket, set my phone and watch to track my miles, and took a deep breath.

Freedom. Fresh air. Mountains all around. I was excited to get on a new trail and run away from politicking and networking. Independence Lake was my destination, located a few miles up the basin on a high alpine shelf surrounded by granite peaks dusted with fresh snow. My shoulders relaxed, and I hit the start button on my watch.

The trail crossed a little stream, and I hopped across a few rocks until the path became a perfect trench of brown dirt tucked in the tundra on both sides. With each step, the power of my movement seemed to push out the pressure to conform and the pretense of my costume suit. I pushed myself up the trail, trying to soak in the grandeur and solitude of the basin, while keeping an eye on the ground for trip hazards. To my left, the slope rose upward to a small shelf holding Lost Man Lake, but that was not my destination.

I pressed onward, watching the sky as clouds billowed and converged into a downy blanket of white and gray. They slid across the summits in a huge mass, drowning out any blue in the sky that had remained. I studied their shape and color, trying to interpret their movement and predict how long it would be, before those giant pillows would fill with moisture and send it dripping to the earth below. The wind carried a damp chill, a clear warning of moisture to come. I felt confident that the clouds skittering across the peaks were just messengers. Distant warning shots of what was to eventually come. I didn't want to turn around, so I picked up the pace.

The cold air burned my lungs, as I breathed in as much oxygen as the 12,000-foot terrain allowed. It was like turning off the switch, entering a zone of lightheadedness and fatigue. I welcomed the familiar suffocating feeling when every breath takes a little more effort.

With each footstep, I felt strong and free. This is where I am. Where I live. Where I am whole. Alone. My body and me. I wished I could stay and enjoy this moment for just a while longer.

The trail became muddy after the previous week's frost and snowmelt. I assumed the lake sat on the bench of rock above and to my right. Yet, there appeared to be another shelf up higher and to the left. I kept on moving, hoping to reach some water before my 50-minute cutoff, and more importantly, before the rain clouds actually delivered precipitation.

Jumping through puddles and mud bogs, I pressed onward toward a flattish spot ahead of me. Soon I saw the gray-blue shimmer of water and shadowy reflections of the peaks. These alpine lakes reminded me of catching fish as a young girl. Water has such power to calm the mind and soothe the soul. These little bodies of water high up in the mountains hold so much beauty in their shining blue and green, and on a cloudy day like today, gray.

I rotated all around to take in the views, as if I were in the rolling green fields of Austria, singing, "The hills are alive . . . " but with the smell of rain and snow. As much as I wanted to linger and even run up to the pass to look over to the other side, I knew that I didn't have the time, nor did the weather have any patience.

I pointed myself back toward the trailhead and let gravity carry my legs down to the car. The view ahead was so stunningly beautiful that I didn't even realize when the mist had started until I saw the ground speckled with wet spots. The smell of damp dirt and the chill in the air meant snow was coming. I picked up my pace, enjoying my solitary run back to the parking lot.

At my car, I looked at the pile of clothes in a heap on the back seat and down at my muddy shoes and smiled. My quick change on a mountain pass had transformed my spirit and freed my soul. Independence Lake was an appropriate destination to mark my transition and honor the new trail I have chosen to run. My days of wearing suits were ending.

I drove back to the city for my last appointment with my career coach. I walked in still wearing my muddy running clothes and proudly announced my resignation.

---

The office grew quiet as people shut down their computers and made their way out of the building. It was past 5 p.m., and I still had to pack up the few personal items scattered on my desk. I also wanted to finish up a few tasks before I could feel good about closing the door behind me.

I added a few more notes to the list of projects, upcoming deadlines, and tasks, and shoved a few more papers into the drawer full of file folders. The rest I tossed into the huge recycling bin occupying the bulk of my office space, now overflowing with 10 years' worth of work. The amount of paper and its disposable nature was a clear reminder of the fleeting impact of one individual in the larger world. Numerous hours went into that big tub, including plenty of reports I'd written and read, notes and tasks from hundreds of meetings, copies of legal statutes and budget analyses, and an alarming number of books and reports I had never even opened. So much of my life energy was heaped in one place, ready to move on and be repurposed.

"Are you still here?" I heard my colleague Wendy ask. "It's your last day. Aren't you supposed to cut out early and not stay late?" she chided.

I chuckled. "I know, I just have a few things I want to do."

"That doesn't surprise me."

"Don't worry, I won't be here long," I reassured her.

Wendy was one of my favorite coworkers, and I would miss her. Like so many others, she told me how much she would miss me. We reminisced about our first days getting to know one another, and all the afternoon runs and peer-mentoring sessions we shared.

I had had a good career. I knew that. And I knew that I wouldn't have been leaving if life had not thrown me a wild curveball. We chatted for a few more minutes until her carpool partner texted that her ride was ready to leave.

I threw the last few papers into the bin, shut the lid, pulled the handle towards me until it balanced on its wheels, and rolled it out into the hallway. My normally cluttered office had been winnowed down to one small box with a few photos, my coffee mug and pink plastic cup, two boxes of business cards—in case I wanted to connect with any of the colleagues filed into the slim containers—and a few of the pens gifted to me at conferences. I took one last swipe with the cleaning cloth across the desk, computer monitor, and keyboard, then tossed it into the trash. I heard the lights click off, and the hallway dimmed. I looked around the office as memories of the previous 10 years flashed before my eyes. I nodded to nothing in particular to acknowledge the past, as I was ready to move on to the future. Slinging my bag over my shoulder, I picked up my box and walked out into the darkening hall and into the stairwell, where a beam of sunlight shone brightly through the skylight. I walked down the two flights of stairs bathed in its soft glow.

## thirteen

## Riding the Tail

*G*ood Luck Runners, the banner read, with the Boston Marathon logo in white lettering with its iconic yellow unicorn on each end. My hand went to my collarbone, feeling the spot where the first lump appeared. My other arm wrapped around my side, sliding up and down my rib cage. Chills shot through me as I realized where I was—Athlete's Village—the start of the Boston Marathon. There were no lumps. It was 2023, 10 years after my diagnosis.

Raindrops splashed off the trash bag I wore to keep dry as I waited in line for the porta-potty. I retrieved my phone, hit the video button, and panned the crowd. There were loads of garbage-bag clad runners clutching water bottles, bananas, and energy bars waiting by a wall of blue toilets. Energy pulsed through every person; it was like standing in a field of static electricity. My whole body tingled as I took in the scene.

The woman on the loudspeaker reminded the crowd, "You are privileged to run in the rain and wind. You earned your spot!" Her fist pumped in the air.

I tried to soak it all in, to take in the full scene and magnitude of this day. A day I never imagined would happen. I was running the Boston Marathon.

---

After I had left my job, I ran another marathon, convinced I could shave 2 minutes from my finishing time and finally qualify for Boston. My sabbatical seemed the perfect time to train, since I no longer had to fit long runs in before work, and was healthy again. I believed my fairy-tale ending was finally being written. It was meant to be. *Five years after a stage four cancer diagnosis, she comes back to crush the course.*

The first 10 miles that day felt great, but at about mile 11 my stomach started gurgling, and my guts exploded at the halfway mark. I had to make three pit stops before crossing the finish line. I could blame it on the spicier-than-expected pasta sauce the night before, but I knew it was my anxiety and ego that got in the way. Not to mention my unorthodox training plan.

Fairy tales don't happen in real life. I wasn't entitled to run the Boston Marathon just because I beat some nasty cancer.

The defeat killed my dream. I was 44 years old and figured my best running years were over. I tossed my running shoes in the back of the closet and said goodbye to Boston. I settled for my cancer victory and relinquished my running goals.

---

As my sabbatical year came to close, I started feeling the pressure to figure out my next job.

"You should be a coach," my friend said one afternoon, after I had listened to her talk about her job and asked questions about her desire to do something different.

"Yeah, right," I quipped.

"No, really. You're always helping me figure out what I should do."

"You're the one figuring it out. I just ask a lot of questions!"

"Exactly."

I didn't think much about her comment. Two weeks later, another friend suggested I go into life coaching.

I knew my career coach made an enormous impact on my life. I also knew that I wanted to give others the gift of insight that my illness gave me. A few weeks later, I signed up for a coaching certification course and immediately realized that I'd found a fit for my leadership experience and interpersonal skills. I then joined the local coaching association, and decided to attend their monthly meetings.

I signed up for several more coaching courses to learn the art and science of coaching, and how people make transformative changes in their life. The more I learned about neuroscience and trauma, the more I understood how the brain adapts and creates behavior patterns based on our experiences. I saw clearly that my transformation was due to how my brain adapted after my illness. Before my diagnosis, I operated out of a lifelong belief that self-sacrifice and overachieving were the direct route to success. That any feelings were to be ignored. When I got sick, I held so much stress inside, and I realized how much that sacrifice cost me. Facing my mortality gave me the courage and urgency to live like I had only wished of living—strong and free. I ignored the advice to rest and continued hiking. I stopped rescuing my boss. I said no to the initial promotion offer, and then declined requests to remain in my job. I was saying no to what I didn't want, and saying yes to who I really was. I listened to my colleagues process their grief after each coworker passed. I sat with John and his family during his final days. I was showing up as me, and slowly rewriting my old beliefs into a new story.

I began to understand the science behind my stories, and realized that I had a clearer idea of how I learned to write my own script. This helped me see how I could help others make transformative changes without facing a life-threatening illness or other crises. My experience taught me how to listen to my inner wisdom, and I knew I could help others do the same, especially those who felt trapped in an endless cycle of self-sacrifice and conformity.

I wanted to be the coach that I wish I had when I interviewed for the job working for my difficult boss. A coach could've helped me see that I had more options than continuing to tolerate a dysfunctional and disrespectful work culture. I was worth more than that. I wanted to be like my career coach who helped me believe what I knew to be true about myself, but was too afraid to admit. My being is as valuable as my doing. I wanted to help others speak their truth and shine their light. "Helping the 'yes' people say 'yes' to themselves," as one client suggested for my slogan. I'd found my second career, and it didn't require bending over backwards, compromising my integrity, or maintaining a purely cognitive approach to life. I could be real—in fact, my value to my clients requires nothing less.

---

After I left my job, Alan and I began searching for a new home away from the city. We drove hundreds of miles, scouring many mountainside communities hoping to find the perfect spot. I wanted open space and a view; Alan dreamed of living in a forest. We shared a desire to be able to hike from our front door. We saw things we liked, but never did more than look.

Then came the pandemic. Mountain communities shut down, and some disallowed visitors. I felt like a caged animal locked in the noisy city. On our first hike after the lockdown, I stepped out of our truck and just stood and listened. Other than a few birds chirping, I heard only silence.

"Oh my gosh, how I've missed this."

"It's glorious," Alan agreed.

I looked around, absorbing the sights and sounds of the forest, and took a deep breath. I savored every step— even the extra walking when I inevitably made a wrong turn. We saw no one on the trail. As we neared the tree line, the views opened to the east until we were on the summit knoll with views in every direction. Tears stung my eyes. I walked over to Alan, wrapped my arms around his waist, and squeezed tight. *We need to move,* I thought.

We finally got serious about house searching, and put bids on a few places only to have them fall through. The real estate market was crazy, so we had to act fast. Eventually, we found a house 6 hours from Denver. It would mean leaving our community of friends, the place where we'd both established our careers, and moving to a place where we knew no one. It was perfect.

Moving from the city to the mountains felt like I was being planted in a verdant garden; my soul was finally allowed to sprout and bloom. I could look outside and see towering ponderosa pines and Gambel oak trees. Mother Nature and the healing power of the outdoors were now outside my door, instead of hours away after fighting traffic. I told friends that it felt like pulling on a favorite pair of old jeans, the ones that are broken in just right and fit perfectly. It was the easiest transition among the dozens of moves that I'd made as an adult.

---

I joined a local running club so I could feel more comfortable running the trails while making new friends. I surrounded myself with super-fit people, and met women who were accomplishing amazing goals—and who were regular people like me. My younger sister finished third overall female in a 100-kilometer race, and I thought of all our shared runs at the farm, and the 50K we did the previous summer. It all tapped into my long-sought-after goal of qualifying for the Boston Marathon. If others could achieve such amazing feats, why couldn't I?

The desire to try again, to see what I was made of, wouldn't go away. A few months later in February 2022, I sat in my chair overlooking our forested yard and opened my laptop. I quickly found the link to the Colorado Marathon registration site, and saw that they still had spots available for their May race. It was the same course I had run in 2013 with all my lumps, and the same course that ended in defeat during my sabbatical. It was just 12 weeks before race day. Normally, I'd follow a 16-week training plan, but I assumed I was in good enough shape to cram it into 12 weeks. I hit Submit on the registration form webpage.

The length of training didn't scare me, but the intensity did. I knew I had to work much harder to finish under the requisite time—and my previous training strategies obviously hadn't worked. A quick search for "marathon training to finish in under 3:45" resulted in a list of links and several articles. I scrolled through the workouts and key tips, and my stomach tightened. Every week included detailed speed sessions with specific pace times and hill workouts on alternating weeks. Five days of running.

I'd never really run speedwork sessions or hill repeats other than sporadic sprints. I had also not been running 5 days a week. Fear crept in, smothering my flame of excitement. I didn't think my body could handle the miles listed on the plan. When I asked myself what the worst thing was that could happen in the training, thoughts of getting injured grew into worries that I could pass out and die. That I wouldn't be able to breathe and would collapse.

It sounded ludicrous, but I started to become aware that I held my breath a lot, or took short and shallow breaths. During a breath-awareness meditation that I had followed, I could barely see my belly rise and fall as the mindfulness teacher described. It was a little disturbing but definitely eye-opening. I thought about my younger years when I sucked in my stomach, never allowing myself to fully exhale as I worried about how fat I might look.

*How does one screw up breathing?* I wondered.

---

Running had been my escape from pain. I ran that hot summer day when I was 11 years old because I didn't know how to deal with the agonizing emotions as I feared for my sister's life. I ran when boyfriends broke up with me, and when I received the rejection letter for a teaching scholarship I so desperately wanted. I ran through college when I felt fat, when my eating was so messed up. Running was my safe place. And now I was telling myself to go run—run faster and harder than I ever had, past the 20-mile threshold at a pace I'd never been able to sustain before. I was telling myself to run *into* the pain.

Panic rose in my chest as I thought about it. The same thought of passing out or suffocating made me anxious.

Closing my eyes, I tried to calm down. Soon, I imagined my teenage self, with my 80's perm perfectly coiffed with hairspray, wearing a favorite fuchsia top with shoulder pads—the same shirt I wore that awful night to the party. She had her arms crossed across her chest, with an angry look in her eye. *She* was afraid of the pain.

I shuddered, not expecting *that* image to be the one that came to mind. I realized that the memory of that fateful night could keep me from my running goals. But as I thought about my teenage self and recalled the pain of that experience, I knew why she was afraid.

I felt sorry for my younger self, wanting to tell her it was OK. I wrote in my journal as if I were writing a letter to that teenage self, reassuring her that we could do this. I told her it would be all right; I would be with her. I would keep her safe. This pain is not the same.

I finally recognized how amazing and strong I had been as that young woman. I had achieved every audacious goal that I had ever set. The protective shield I had developed had given me the strength to travel and experience the world, and to rise into leadership roles. She was me, and we were so powerful.

I saw that the walls I had built over the years were not just dividers that had separated me from the world, but they also served as a ladder into a place I could never have otherwise entered. The struggles and pressures I had felt served a purpose—to bring me here. The same strength that allowed me to move on from my small town also allowed me to push through my treatments. Beneath the bcrating self-talk was a fierce desire to live and love myself. That same commitment showed up in every plea not to die.

I sat in my chair astonished at this revelation. I stayed with this image, allowing my younger self to say what she needed to say, to voice the words I wished I could have said 30 years ago, and to feel the support of another human being.

After I opened my eyes, I found myself looking around the room to see if anyone was there. Our conversation felt so vivid and powerful. I felt my shoulders relax, and my jaw loosen.

It was a breakthrough moment. I understood how I learned to freeze and hold my breath to endure pain; it was my protective response. I didn't fully understand how this played out in my running, but if my fear of pain was keeping me from pushing beyond my current limits, I wanted to overcome it.

Between the speedwork runs and adding dedicated breathing exercises to my plan, I coined my Boston qualifying training my great "pain experiment." I was going to learn to push through it, or find my limits trying.

I had treated my body as if it were the beat-up car that I'd driven in high school—capable and dependable but not flashy. What if my body were more like a sports car—fast and sleek? What if I had underestimated my physical abilities all along? I began picturing myself as a lean marathoner, sprinting down the track.

I was no longer running away from myself but running *toward* myself. I was going out purposely to feel my body and its power. To be in my body and my mind, at the same time. It was a connection I hadn't fully made in the past.

Before each long run, I set a learning goal. On a 14-mile run I committed to being curious about my sports car abilities. *Go out and feel the strength and wisdom of your body,* I told myself.

I felt great and kept my desired pace for the first 6 miles. When I hit the steep hill at about the halfway point, I could feel myself slowing, while I calculated how many more miles I had to go. The usual excuses starting rolling through my head, telling me I could slow down—it was a hill and just a training run. I was hitting my usual breaking point, when my mind gave me a convenient reason to slow down, take a walk break, or just complain.

I looked down at my legs and asked, "What do you want to do?"

For the first time, I *felt* my legs, and they were fine, much better than my mind had me believe. I'd been running for over 30 years, but had not once really asked my body anything. I remembered my first run on the gravel road when I looked down at my sweaty legs, and saw the muscles contracting and expanding. It was as if they were telling me, *let's go, girl—what are you waiting for?* My stride lengthened, and I easily strode to the top of the hill. I ran the next 7 miles with a smile on my face—and faster than my goal pace. I had found the key to unlock my fear of pain. It had been my mind that had been holding me back in the past, not my body.

I thought I'd healed the psychological wounds of the past through therapy and other counseling. This experience taught me about the power of our physical selves and the body-brain connection. Like my tumors screaming at me to stop sacrificing my talents, my legs shouted to keep moving. My body was no longer just flesh and blood, muscle, and bones, but a living, breathing powerful being. And a being I could trust.

By the time I stood at the starting line for my qualifying race, I was ready to run. I wasn't worried about my time goal; I knew I had already won my race. Runners talk about their "BQ"—their Boston Qualifying race. My BQ was a Body Quest—a journey to discover the power and strength of my physical self and my mind's ability to overcome its past patterns. The race wasn't about a fairy-tale ending or tidy bookend, and I wasn't relying on angels or fairy dust to magically make me run fast.

The first 10 miles went by quickly as I chatted with others in the pace group. My gut did its usual rumbling near the 12-mile mark, but I had built in time for a pit stop, so I sprinted to the bathrooms, and then got back on the course. Keeping my pacer, the runner in the neon-green shirt who was setting the pace for my desired finish time, within my sights, I ran alone for the remainder of the race, all the while feeling the strength of my legs and focusing on my breathing.

My intestines barely held on for the second half, but I was able to shift into that new gear and found my zone through the last 6 miles of mental and physical anguish. When I rounded the last corner and glimpsed the finish line, knowing I was well ahead of my goal time, I felt a surge of energy course through my legs, as I let them carry me to the timing mat.

My emotions grew with each stride, and I pumped my arms and gave one last sprint to the red carpet. I threw my hands up in victory, and hobbled to the woman who placed the finisher medal around my neck.

I finished 6½ minutes faster than my qualifying time. And nearly 10 minutes faster than my first attempt, with all my lumps.

My heart thumped, as my chest heaved from pure exhaustion and adrenaline. Deep breaths turned into sobs as I walked toward the trash bin to keep from falling over. Tears of joy flowed down my cheeks as the emotions of the last 9 years of my life rushed out—fighting to survive and somehow beating the odds, finding love and a new career, and reconnecting with my amazing body. Alan came over and wrapped his arms around me, and we both cried into each other's shoulders, our joy and love entwined with sweaty arms and salty tears.

*I did it. I qualified for Boston. I am alive.*

Four months later, I received the coveted acceptance into the Boston Marathon. I stood in the kitchen reading and rereading the words. Chills ran through my entire body, and my muscles turned to rubber. I had to sit down. And write. I tapped at my keyboard, fingers shaking, trying to capture the moment and its emotions. *"Not bawling my eyes out like I did at the finish line. No tears yet; although I feel them coming as I sit here, on this 5-year anniversary of John's death as I ponder the fact that not only am I alive, but I AM RUNNING THE \*!@#$% BOSTON MARATHON!!!"*

When I realized the date and its significance, I looked up to the heavens and thanked my Lucky Johnny for all he had done for me. *I get to run 26.2 miles*, I told him. *I wish you could come cheer me on and wave that hat of yours in the air.*

When I started packing my suitcase for Boston, laying out multiple options of tops and bottoms to fit various weather conditions, I felt a tingly sensation all over my body unlike anything I'd ever experienced. It wouldn't go away. But it wasn't like the nerves I'd felt in other races or before big presentations that made my stomach churn. It was like an electric current running from my head down to my toes. It felt like every nerve ending was awake and sending out its feelers, and the air itself caused them to react.

That tingly feeling stayed with me on the airplane, and after we landed and walked through the Boston Common and over to Faneuil Hall. I felt it on our way to the convention center to pick up my bib and race packet. There was a lightness to it, almost a floating sensation. My senses were in overdrive, taking in the sights and sounds and people around me.

I woke early on race morning, and tried to drink my coffee and eat my banana bread as I fretted about which top to wear. The forecast called for rain and cool temperatures. I was barely finished with my breakfast when I received a text from Gina, my friend and running partner, saying she was on her way. Time seemed to pass in slow motion, and at Mach speed at the same time. The first two hours of race morning were already over, but I felt like the morning alarm had just gone off.

Our start time wasn't for 3 hours, but we needed to drop off our bags and get on the bus that would take us to the start line. The minute I walked out into the street, the energy pulsed as thousands of runners walked the streets and milled about.

I followed Gina as she led the way to drop off our bags at the finish line, staying close on her heels so we did not get separated. Trying not to trip or bump into someone, I looked around in awe as we moved with the sea of runners down the street. I could hardly believe that I was part of this crowd, this event, and that I would experience it firsthand. Finding the bus that corresponded to my bib number, I walked to the table and gave my bag to the volunteer, who reminded me to come back to bus number 25. I looked at the sign in the window and smiled; 25 is my lucky number.

I wasn't prepared for the energy and vibe of 30,000 runners who'd worked as hard as I had to get to this race, and what that collective energy and enthusiasm and commitment would feel like. Maybe everyone was walking around feeling like a Fourth-of-July sparkler, and our individual flickers were colliding into a massive fireworks display.

I floated along with the crowd, smiling at the young women singing Taylor Swift songs at the top of their lungs, and an older man and woman comparing injury lists and race locations. Organizers expertly guided us to the buses that would take us to the start line. I was grateful for the guidance; all the electricity fried my brain and I could hardly remember my name.

Gina and I swapped stories as the bus made its way out of Boston to Hopkinton. Soon, we were engulfed by masses of people making their way to a corral of porta-potties encircling the large schoolyard. Rain fell steadily, so we pulled on our trash-bag coats, as my toes started to numb in my cold wet shoes. We slowly made our way through the swarms of runners, and walked the many blocks towards the Start line. My body still tingled, as I half-worried that I wouldn't be able to run.

We stopped at the last corral of porta-potties, and decided to ditch our rain gear and the extra layers we were wearing to keep warm. Volunteers graciously accepted my old sweatshirt and the blue navy sweatpants. As I handed them to the volunteer, I realized they were my old PET scan pants. We kept walking, me in my tingly stupor waiting for tears—instead, a wide silly grin stayed plastered on my face as we made our way to the Start and began running. We passed by the starting clock, as I was still trying to comprehend that I was actually running in the Boston Marathon. My body seemed to float above the pavement as we dodged puddles of rain and weaved between runners. People cheered, some even with beer in their hands. I giggled at the sign in a yard around Mile 2, "You're almost there—not." I couldn't believe the number of people out on their lawns, lining the streets, clapping, and yelling, despite the cold, damp weather.

I smiled through the downpour at Mile 13, grinning at the young women and their cheeky signs in the Wellesley College "Scream Tunnel." I could hear their cheering well before we hit campus, the noise sending shivers down my spine. Scream Tunnel was definitely an accurate description.

I did the "YMCA" moves every time I heard it blaring from someone's loudspeakers. The music was a highlight. Neil Diamond's "Sweet Caroline" became my favorite of the day. The only tears I shed along the course were happy ones. I shed a few for my brother when Toto's "Africa" played. That tune always took me back to our childhood home, recording songs off the radio in his bedroom. He had died unexpectedly in 2019, but I felt his spirit pushing me, just as when we were younger and he'd egg me on to play one more round of HORSE basketball. Mumford & Son's "I Will Wait" played around the halfway point and made me think of Alan, and how lucky I was to have him in my life.

The miles ticked by effortlessly, and we entered the hilly portion of the course. I kept a steady pace, and let the crowd's energy push me up the incline. I got so lost in watching the spectators and taking in the parade-like atmosphere that I missed a few mile markers. Somehow, we were already at Mile 20, and I was still floating on a cloud.

I hadn't looked at my watch, as I'd made a promise to myself to simply enjoy the race and not worry about finish times. With just a few miles to go, curiosity got the best of me, and I glanced down at my watch, wondering just how slow we were going. I didn't feel winded or tired, and my belly barely rumbled. I started to calculate our estimated finish time, and didn't believe my math. It was a dream race. The most perfect and easy 26.2 miles I had ever run. I wanted to keep going, to stay in that moment and feel the energy of the crowd.

The course passed Fenway Park, and I saw Alan along with Gina's mom, and a friend of ours, cheering us on the sidelines. Only 1 mile remained. Gina and I made the final turn onto Boylston Street, as the roar of the crowd grew. I could see the finish line and the time clock. I started running faster, hoping we could finish in under 3:50. The final blocks felt longer than any portion of the race, as I watched the seconds tick on the clock. I matched my stride with Gina so we could finish together, and we raised our hands as our feet landed on the timing mat. I hit the button on my watch. 3:49:18, which ended up being our official finish time. Our time qualified us to apply to come back next year!

Gina and I hugged and high-fived, and I hugged her again. My body shook, as I closed my eyes.

"You can cry now," Gina whispered in my ear. I had warned her that I might cry my way through the entire race.

"Oh my gosh, that was amazing! Wow! I still can't believe I am here. Oh my gosh! Thank you for running with me," I told her as I squeezed tightly.

There were no tears. I had shed them all on my journey to arrive at this place. I felt only pure joy and gratitude. My healing complete. Body, mind, and heart reunited. Rejoicing.

# Acknowledgments

This book started as a way to answer the question of "What just happened to me?" It morphed from pages documenting important moments, places and people that stood out in my mind, to a nagging voice that said it needed to go beyond my computer. Someone needed to read it. I hope my story helps someone in the same way so many others' stories have helped me.

I owe more than I can ever pay to Karen Gulliver, the kindest editor who is responsible for turning my snippets into stories, and flashbacks into foundational memories. Thank you for helping me dig deeper to give a fuller picture of the story. You were my voice of reason, and you taught me when it was appropriate to let my sailor mouth run free.

I also want to thank Emily Barrosse, Christine O'Connor, and the entire team at Bold Story Press for their patience, and for shepherding me through the process and always answering my million questions and requests.

Of course, I should have started by thanking my doctors who have given their energy and brilliance to melanoma research and treatment and ultimately saved my life. Dr. Rene Gonzalez, you will always be my hero and favorite Plague Doctor. Dr. Lala Cornelius, the first time we met you emanated hope, and I always trusted you had my best interests in mind. My dermatologist, Dr. Joanna Burch, your voicemail just days after my diagnosis made me feel seen in the wild world of medicine I was entering. I miss our appointments and will never find another as kind as you. Thank you to all the nurses and medical professionals who give their lives in service to others.

There aren't words to fully encapsulate the gratitude I feel for John Foley and his presence in my life. This one is for you, Lucky Johnny. I wish you were my co-author and not my dedication line. And to Janice and the Foley family—what a gift you are to me and Alan. This story would not be whole without you.

I also want to thank some people I've never met but nonetheless shaped this book. Marion Roach Smith, I took your memoir classes and listen to all your podcasts, and you helped me discover my argument. It's about crisis and letting it break you open instead of break you down. And Jeff Goins, who also taught me valuable writing tools, most notably how to capture the dilemma and the decision in every scene that made it to this book.

To my parents, my first role models of resiliency, hope, and love. Thank you to my brother for sharing his fearless spirit with his scaredy cat sister, and for teaching me the power of forgiveness. To all my sisters, for being the strong, beautiful women you are. Thank you to all my family and friends who have encouraged and patiently waited for me to write it all down. Your support through all of life's ups and downs means more than I can express.

Thank you, Gina Denten, for all the running miles, showing me how to run Boston and for reading my early crap draft. To Jolene, for reviewing the final drafts and helping me get over my mental blocks to sharing my story. To everyone who has read my ramblings on various platforms. Thank you for encouraging me to write, even if you were lying.

And I really would not be here without my husband, Alan, whose love gave me a reason to hope and desire to grow old with someone. Thank you for being my forever cheerleader and adventure companion. I love you with all my heart.

# About the Author

Raised on a farm in Iowa, Rochelle has always enjoyed the outdoors. She received degrees from Marquette and DePaul universities in social welfare and leadership and spent twenty years leading public policy and nonprofit efforts to advance economic opportunity.

She lives in Colorado where she is a writer and life coach, helping perfectionists and overachievers find balance and avoid burnout. Finzel is happiest running, biking, hiking, skiing, and sharing nature's wonders with her husband.

# About Bold Story Press

**BOLD STORY PRESS**

Bold Story Press is a woman-owned, hybrid publishing company with a mission of publishing women writers so that their stories contribute to shaping the narrative of our world. Join our community and help us to build a world where every woman's voice is celebrated.

At Bold Story Press, we believe in the transformative power of women's stories. Our mission is to empower women to create narratives, break barriers, and shape the world through their voices.

We believe that when women's voices are heard, the world becomes a better place. Imagine a world where women are equally represented as decision-makers, influencers, and leaders in politics, corporate America, the media, and the arts. At Bold Story Press, we envision a future where diversity in leadership is not a goal but a reality. Our commitment is to provide a platform that celebrates, amplifies, and honors the diverse experiences of women.

The Bold Story Press logo, designed by Grace Arsenault, was inspired by the nom de plume, or pen name, a sad necessity at one time for female authors who wanted to publish. The woman's face hidden in the quill is the profile of Virginia Woolf, who, in addition to being an early feminist writer, founded and ran her own publishing company, Hogarth Press.

www.ingramcontent.com/pod-product-compliance
Lightning Source LLC
Chambersburg PA
CBHW071409090426
42737CB00011B/1399